Rhinegold Study Guides

A Student's Guide to Music Technology

for the **Edexcel** AS and A2 Specification

by
Bruce Cole
Andy Collyer
David M Howard
Andy Hunt and
Damian Murphy

R·

Rhinegold Publishing Ltd
241 Shaftesbury Avenue
London WC2H 8TF
Telephone: 01832 270333
Fax: 01832 275560
www.rhinegold.co.uk

Rhinegold Study Guides
(music series editor: Paul Terry)

A Student's Guide to GCSE Music for the Edexcel Specification
Listening Tests for Students (Books 1 and 2): Edexcel GCSE Music Specification
A Student's Guide to AS Music for the Edexcel Specification
Listening Tests for Students (Books 1 and 2): Edexcel AS Music Specification
A Student's Guide to A2 Music for the Edexcel Specification
Listening Tests for Students (Books 1 and 2): Edexcel A2 Music Specification

Similar books have been produced for the AQA and OCR Music Specifications. Also available are:

A Student's Guide to GCSE Music for the WJEC Specification (separate English and Welsh language versions)
A Student's Guide to AS/A2 Music Technology for the Edexcel AS and A2 Specification
AS/A2 Listening Tests for Music Technology

The following books are designed to support all GCSE and GCE music courses:

A Student's Guide to Composing (Book 1 for GCSE and Book 2 for A-level Music)
A Student's Guide to Harmony and Counterpoint (for AS and A2 Music)

Other Rhinegold Study Guides

Students' Guides to AS and A2 Drama and Theatre Studies for the AQA and Edexcel Specifications
Students' Guides to AS and A2 Performance Studies for the OCR Specification
Students' Guides to AS and A2 Religious Studies for the AQA, Edexcel and OCR Specifications

Rhinegold Publishing also publishes Classical Music, Classroom Music, Early Music Today, Music Teacher,
Opera Now, Piano, Teaching Drama, The Singer, British and International Music Yearbook,
British Performing Arts Yearbook, Music Education Yearbook, Rhinegold Dictionary of Music in Sound.

First published 2001 in Great Britain by
Rhinegold Publishing Limited
241 Shaftesbury Avenue
London WC2H 8TF
Telephone: 01832 270333
Fax: 01832 275560
www.rhinegold.co.uk
Reprinted 2002, New Edition 2003, Reprinted 2004, New Edition 2005

© Rhinegold Publishing Limited 2001, 2005

You should always check the current requirements of the examination, since these may change.
Copies of the Edexcel Specification may be obtained from Edexcel Examinations at
Edexcel Publications, Adamsway, Mansfield, Notts. NG18 4FN
Telephone 01623 467467, Facsimile 01623 450481, Email publications@linneydirect.com
See also the Edexcel website at http://www.edexcel.org.uk/

A Student's Guide to Music Technology for the Edexcel AS and A2 Specification
British Library Cataloguing in Publication Data.
A catalogue record for this book is available from the British Library.
ISBN 0-904226-25-6
Printed in Great Britain by WPG Ltd

Wee have also Sound-houses, wher we practise and demonstrate all Sounds, and their Generation. Wee have harmonies which you have not, of Quarter-Sounds, and lesser Slides of Sounds. Diverse Instruments of Musick likewise to you unknowne, some sweeter than any you have; Together with Bells and Rings that are dainty and sweet. Wee represent Small Sounds as well as Great and Deepe; Likewise Great Sounds, Extenuate and Sharpe; Wee make diverse Tremblings and Warblings of Sounds, which in their Originalle are Entire. Wee represent and imitate all Articulate Sounds and Letters, and the Voices and Notes of Beasts and Birds. Wee have certain Helps, which sett to the Eare doe further the Hearing greatly. Wee have also diverse Strange and Artificiall Echos's, Reflecting the Voice many times, and as it were Tossing it: And some that give back the Voice lowder than it come, some Shriller, some Deeper; Yea some rendering the Voice, Differing in the letters or Articulate Sound, from that they receyve, Wee have also means to convey Sounds in Trunks and Pipes, in strange Lines, and Distances.

Francis Bacon (*The New Atlantis*, published 1627)

Contents

The authors

Bruce Cole is fellow in community music at the University of York, principal examiner in composition to Edexcel and has been a scrutineer for the Qualifications and Curriculum Authority. He has taught at most levels from preschool to postgraduate including PGCE, and his work as a composer includes rock musicals, orchestral commissions and scores for film, TV, theatre and dance. He is the author of *The Composer's Handbook*, the co-author (with David Bowman) of *Sound Matters* and a member of the editorial board of *Music Education Research*. Current projects include a handbook for schools on composing popular music and a teaching research programme with postgraduate teachers and young offenders.

Andy Collyer has been principal examiner for Edexcel's AS music technology and is a lecturer, performer and composer. He has been closely linked with new music technology and popular music qualifications (including GCE Music Technology) and has been involved in examining and assessment for a number of years. In addition to his classical music training, Andy has an abiding interest and experience in all forms of popular music and musical theatre, where he has been a performer and composer for many years, working on music, theatre and music technology projects in Liverpool, all over the South West and in London, often with young people. Andy is also a reviewer for *Music Teacher* magazine and a committed music technology educationalist.

Professor David M Howard holds a personal chair in music technology in the department of electronics at the University of York. His teaching interests include acoustics and psychoacoustics, human speech and singing production, as well as the analysis and synthesis of singing, speech and music. In his research David is interested in the measurable effects of professional training on human voice production and the potential for the use of computers in voice teaching in the future. He is also interested in new methods of synthesising singing, speech and music as well as physical modelling of acoustic spaces. David has played keyboard (mainly pipe organs and synthesisers) for many years, and sung in choirs. He currently conducts the Beningbrough Singers, a group of 13 singers who perform mainly sacred and secular *a capella* works, and he is an occasional lay clerk (tenor) at Ripon Cathedral. He co-authored *Acoustics and Psychoacoustics* with James Angus, which was specially written to give those interested in music technology a practical and musical introduction to acoustics and psychoacoustics.

Dr Andy Hunt is a lecturer in music and media technology at the University of York. He teaches electronic musical instruments, MIDI, computer programming and special needs technology. His PhD focused on improving the user interface for electronic musical instruments. This has led to a range of research interests that involve the application of novel interfacing techniques to problems in medical, computing and artistic fields. He is the inventor of the *MidiGrid* computer music software, co-developer of the *MIDAS Multimedia Toolkit*, and the author of a number of publications including the music technology textbook *Digital Sound Processing for Music and MultiMedia*.

Dr Damian Murphy is a lecturer in the Department of Electronics at the University of York, specialising in music technology and recording studio techniques. Previously he has held positions in the School of Music at Bretton Hall College and Leeds Metropolitan University where he helped to establish a new music technology degree course in the School of Engineering. He also acts as sector adviser and external verifier for the NCFE vocational awarding body in the area of media and performing arts and has worked as a consultant for the Qualifications and Curriculum Authority in the area of music technology. His research interests include physical modelling techniques in musical acoustics, sound spatialisation, and digital signal processing as applied to creative audio processing. He is an advocate of the use of music technology in education and as an access tool to creativity, and has run a number of introductory workshops based around this popular field. Damian is also a keen composer and musician (guitar as his main instrument), working in the fields of contemporary computer music and electronica. He is also a member of the Sightsonic organising committee for York's annual digital-arts festival.

The editor

Paul Terry was formerly a chief examiner in music for Edexcel, for whom he pioneered the first UK A-level award in music technology in the 1990s. He has been a music examiner for more than 20 years and has worked as a consultant to several examination boards as well as serving as a member of such bodies as the Secondary Examinations Council. His publications include many books on aspects of A-level music and he is series editor of the *Study Area* section of *Music Teacher* magazine. He is co-author with William Lloyd of *Music in Sequence, a complete guide to MIDI sequencing* (1991), *Classics in Sequence* (1992) and *Rock in Sequence* (1996).

Acknowledgements

The authors would like to thank Andrew Kitchenham, chief examiner in A-level Music Technology for Edexcel, for his advice in the preparation of this book. Nevertheless if any errors have been made these are the responsibility of the authors. We would also like to thank Dr Lucien Jenkins, Abigail Walmsley and Ann Barkway for their help in the preparation of this guide.

Websites

Addresses of websites given in this guide are believed to be correct at the time of publication, but note that these can change or be withdrawn without notice.

A website for this guide is maintained by one of its authors at: **http://www.york.ac.uk/inst/mustech/as_mustech.htm**

This includes links to the sites mentioned in this guide – clicking on these will save you having to type out the addresses. The intention is to publish additional supporting information there from time to time.

Introduction

Course overview

This book is intended to help you with your study for Edexcel's AS and A2 Music Technology examinations. You will find tips, hints and information covering all aspects of the course.

Let's begin by looking at what you have to cover. The AS and A2 units each consist of three parts (two coursework and one timed examination) all of which are linked to the areas of study outlined below. Your teacher will give you a deadline for coursework – note that this is likely to be before 15 May in the examination year.

AS Music Technology

Three areas of study underpin work for the AS unit, the first of which also runs throughout the A2 unit:

+ the development of music technology
+ music from the western classical tradition
+ popular music and jazz.

You will need to complete the following three components. The first accounts for 40% of the marks for AS Music Technology and the other two are weighted at 30% each.

Sequencing or Recording

You will study **either** sequencing **or** recording and produce two pieces of coursework. If you specialise in recording, you will record a classical piece direct to two-track **and** a piece of popular music or jazz using multitrack and close-mic techniques. If you specialise in sequencing you will sequence a classical piece **and** a pop or jazz piece from scores. In both cases you will have to keep a logbook outlining your processes and use of equipment, and complete a structured commentary on the classical piece you have chosen.

Arranging and Improvising Using Technology

This part also requires two tasks. The first is to produce your own arrangement of a classical, pop or jazz melody. This has to be submitted in the form of a score and parts, which must be produced using a computer, along with a recording on CD or mini-disc.

For the second task you must produce an improvised arrangement of a pop or jazz piece using either sequencing or studio-based technology (if you chose sequencing for the Sequencing or Recording unit you should use recording technology for this task, but if you chose recording then you should use sequencing here). Your finished arrangement must be recorded on CD or mini-disc but you are not required to produce a score or parts for this arrangement.

You will also have to submit a commentary for both of these tasks detailing use of equipment and your musical intention.

Listening and Analysing I

The final part of the AS exam is the written paper. You will be given a CD with extracts of music from a range of periods and genres and will be asked questions concerning the musical, stylistic and technological features of the extracts. This exam will have a mixture of multiple-choice, short answer and essay questions.

A2 Music Technology

The areas of study on which the A2 unit is based are:

✦ the development of music technology
✦ **either** *Music for the Moving Image* **or** *Words and Music*.

You will need to complete the following three components. Each of the first two accounts for 30% of the marks for the A2 unit while the third is weighted at 40%.

Sequencing, Recording and Producing

This component involves **three** coursework tasks. Firstly, you will make a close-mic, multitrack recording of popular music, using at least four tracks. Secondly, you will sequence a backing track using a MIDI workstation. This can be in any style. Thirdly, you add between two and four live tracks to your sequenced backing, at least one of which must be a vocal track.

Composing Using Technology

You will have to produce **two** compositions, one of which can be in any style and for which you or your teacher can set the brief. For the second you will have to work to a brief set by Edexcel – you will be able to choose either a topic related to *Music for the Moving Image* or one related to *Words and Music*. You can submit the compositions in the form of a score or just as a recording.

Listening and Analysing II

In the first part of this written paper you will be given a score plus a CD-ROM containing audio and MIDI files of the same music. You will be asked to compare the recordings and score, comment on certain aspects of the music, identify errors in the MIDI file and identify ways in which the MIDI data could be changed or improved. The second part of the paper will be based on extracts of music you have analysed as part of your chosen area of study – either *Music for the Moving Image* or *Words and Music*. You will, as for AS, be asked questions concerning the musical, stylistic and technological features of the extracts on the audio CD but your answers will be in continuous prose.

Using this guide

The first part of this book deals with getting started and is followed by an introduction to the development of music technology. The chapters on recording and sequencing include the requirements for both the AS and A2 courses, and explain how these differ. We next discuss the skills you need for arranging (AS) and composing (A2). Finally we look at the requirements of the AS and A2 papers in Listening and Analysis. At the end of the book you will find a glossary. When an important technical term is used for the first time in the guide it is printed in **bold type** to indicate that it can be looked-up in this glossary. Sections of the book headed 'Private study' are designed to help you check your understanding of what you have read – many of the answers should be clear by carefully rereading the preceding paragraphs or checking the glossary.

Helpful practice material for the listening tests is given in *AS/A2 Listening Tests for Music Technology* by Andy Collyer, Rhinegold Publishing Ltd, ISBN 1-904226-45-0. Workbook and Audio CD, each available separately.

The details of the specification are believed to be correct at the time of going to press, but you and your teachers should always check current requirements for the examination with Edexcel, since these may change.

Before you start

Before beginning this course it would be wise to look at the two words 'music' and 'technology'. Both are equally important.

You will need to be able to use a combination of technology and musicianship effectively and creatively to make music – whether it's writing a score, using **MIDI**, a **sampler** or **audio**, or through recording and production techniques. As you have seen from the course overview, you will need both musical and technological skills in order to obtain a good grade in this subject.

You may well find that your current knowledge is more heavily weighted in one direction or the other. You may be a strong musician who has had little experience of making music with technology or you may be a computer wizard (or a genius with the MD8 you have in your bedroom) but have little or no formal musical training. Either way, it's possible to fill in the gaps as you learn on the course.

However it's much better to try to make sure that you have a wide a range of skills and knowledge before you start the course as this will enable you to hit the ground running rather than simply learning on the job. You will have a lot of coursework to complete, and this may not allow as much time as you might like for learning and experimenting.

First list what you can already do. Put a tick in the boxes where the statement applies to you now. You can add ticks as you acquire expertise or understanding and more statements become true.

☐ I can read and write music with ease

☐ I can recognise and understand key signatures, scales and chords

☐ I can recognise the sounds of a range of instruments

☐ I can recognise and describe music from a range of pop and jazz styles throughout the 20th century

☐ I can recognise and describe music from a range of classical styles before the 20th century

☐ I can play a keyboard with some confidence

☐ I can perform on an instrument or voice

☐ I can use sequencing **software** (*Cubase*, *Cakewalk* etc.)

☐ I can use music notation software (*Sibelius*, *Finale* etc.)

☐ I can use a portastudio for recording

☐ I can recognise and describe different effects used on commercial recordings

Bear in mind that not all of the boxes will need to be ticked before you start the course, but aim to fill in as many of the gaps as possible in the early months of your studies.

Music

Let's start by looking at the first word, 'music'. Music makes up at least half of the exam so you will need to be a competent musician. This includes learning about the various conventions involved in music-making, understanding how to produce stylish and effective performances, and developing a keen aural awareness when playing and listening to music. Try to develop all of these aspects of your own musicianship, remembering that technology is there to serve the music, and not the other way round.

You will need to have good basic music skills, which will include reading and writing standard music notation, understanding keys, scales and chords, the ranges of different instruments, transposition and basic music terminology.

There are several ways to raise your skills level. You can opt to teach yourself either online, or with an interactive **CD-ROM** or software. The advantage of teaching yourself the electronic way is that good software or online tutorials allow you to test yourself as you go so that you know what you are learning and what needs further work. Another way is to get some Associated Board music theory workbooks from your school, college or local music shop and work through them. The best way of all, though, is to identify any gaps in your knowledge and then ask your subject teacher for clarification of anything you don't understand. Your teacher won't mind – in fact, they will be delighted if you show an interest in the work and in improving your own performance. Another advantage is that your teacher can explain things in the way you are most likely to understand if you find a concept hard to grasp. Information technology cannot do this for you.

You will need to have an understanding of:
+ pitches in treble and bass clefs
+ note durations and rhythm
+ major and minor scales
+ key signatures
+ time signatures
+ basic articulation marks (**staccato**, accent etc)
+ basic chord structures
+ tempo, dynamics and other performance instructions
+ signs and terms for repeating bars and sections.

If you can get yourself to about the standard of grade 3 theory then this would be a good start for your first year.

Keyboard skills are useful in several ways:

+ Playing a keyboard can help you to understand theory in a very clear way, showing you the pattern of tones and semitones in a scale, the various shapes of chords, and so forth. It's much easier to see these patterns on a keyboard than on a guitar. Shown *right* is a simple G-major chord in notation and in finger positions on a guitar and a keyboard. On a keyboard you can clearly see and count the gap of four semitones between the two lowest notes and the gap of three semitones between the two highest notes. This is much harder to see on the guitar.

Music theory

A good starting point for locating resources about music theory on the WWW is http://cctr.umkc.edu/userx/bhugh/musicold.html

For details of music theory CD-ROMS see:
http://www.musictheory.halifax.ns.ca/
http://www.risingsoftware.com/
http://www.ars-nova.com/
http://www.alfred.com

Note that American musical terminology is used in most of these resources (such as 'measure' rather than 'bar' and 'quarter note' rather than 'crotchet') – although differences of this sort are small and are widely understood by British musicians.

Books on music theory are available from all good music retailers.

Playing a keyboard

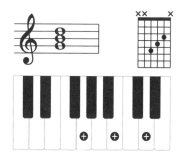

Basic guides to keyboard playing are available from all good music retailers, or go to http://www.musicroom.com/ and follow the links to piano or keyboard music and then click on 'tutor books'.

+ A keyboard is the main method of inputting data into a sequencing package. If you can't play a keyboard at a basic level, you will have to draw or drag and drop all of the notes, which is very time consuming and sounds mechanical. The better your keyboard skills are, the quicker and more musically you can input the data. This will save you a lot of editing in the later stages of producing your sequencing coursework.

+ A keyboard is a very useful tool for composing and arranging, especially when used in conjunction with sequencing software. It allows you to try out chord sequences, melodies and textures.

Listening to music

Strong listening skills are vital to musicians and music technologists alike. For the AS paper in Listening and Analysis, you will need to be able to:

+ recognise musical elements such as melodies, rhythms and chord patterns

+ recognise the sounds of a wide range of instruments

+ identify and describe a range of genres of music (a genre is a category, such as piano sonatas or madrigals)

+ identify and describe the application of recording and performance technology in the music you hear.

How many of the following types of music can you define and recognise?

Acid rock, bebop, britpop, calypso, country, disco, electric folk, funk, fusion, glam rock, goth, heavy metal, hip hop, house, indie, new age, new romantic, progressive rock, punk, rhythm and blues, reggae, rock 'n' roll, salsa, ska, techno, trad jazz, trance, trip hop, two-tone, different types of world music.

The easiest way to build up these skills is to listen to a lot of music. But you must be aware that the music you should listen to most should be unfamiliar and not just the music that you already enjoy. Go through your parents' or grandparents' collection of recordings and try to listen to a variety of music from different periods. You should listen especially for features that help identify the style or date of the piece.

One thing to bear in mind is that you should listen with an open mind. Just because you don't like a certain kind of music doesn't mean that it's bad. It may not appeal to you on the surface but if you listen to it carefully, you may find admirable qualities in terms of performance, production, songwriting or arrangement that you may want to use as part of your coursework.

Technology

This element of the course allows you to put your musical skills into action and be really creative, but first you will need to master the basics. Most of this will be done in lesson time but there's no harm in getting a head start by reading a few of the books listed at the end of this chapter. They will give you a number of ideas and will be a good investment as reference books throughout the course.

Sequencing

Sites for information on MIDI software. Don't forget to shop around.

http://www.midi-classics.com/
http://www.cakewalk.com/
http://www.steinberg.net/
http://www.synthzone.com/
http://www.xdt.com/ar/linux-snd/

This is one area on which you can make a start with limited equipment. Basic sequencing packages are often included on the free disks that come with computer magazines, or can be downloaded from the Internet. Some of these are partially working demos but complete freeware applications are also available, as are moderately priced commercial programs. If you really want to splash out on something bigger and more comprehensive, find out what program is used by your school or college and buy that (you will also need to find out whether the school computers are PC or Mac). This will help with compatibility problems when you transfer work between home and school. You may find that buying the software through your school or college will get you an educational discount. Be prepared to shop around and do not accept the first price you see.

Most MIDI sequencing software operates on similar principles, so any skills you learn on one program can usually be transferred to another. For example, if you are fluent with Cubase, learning Cakewalk or Logic will take you a relatively short time. What you will be learning, no matter which software you use, will be the basic principles of sequencing.

Some software is intended primarily for sequencing and facilities for editing music notation may be limited. Other programs are designed primarily for generating scores and may produce MIDI files that sound lifeless and mechanical. If you want to use a single application (such as Sibelius) that offers both functions, be sure to check out its full range of facilities and remember to ask your teacher for advice.

Good working practices

You should cultivate two important habits when working with technology – they will help prevent much potential anguish.

✦ Save your work frequently. Train your hand to automatically type ctrl+S (or command+S on a Mac) every few minutes. This will take you less than a second and can save hours of time. Many students have worked away for hours and come up with some good sequencing; then the computer crashes and work has been lost. You may not be able to recreate that beautiful sound you just made if you have not immediately saved it.

✦ Always make back-up copies of your work. If you trust all your coursework to a single floppy disk and that disk corrupts or gets lost, you will have to start again. This could happen only days away from your coursework deadline, which may result in you not being able to complete the exam. Save to your hard drive at home and at school, and keep **two** backups, making sure you have updates of both the current and previous work sessions.

Recording

What you can learn about recording prior to starting the course will depend on access to equipment. Don't even think about equipping yourself with a home studio unless you are prepared to spend a fair bit of money and have a fairly large space to set the studio up!

However if you have access to some musicians and to a few mics and a **DAT** or **MD** recorder, you could use the information in some of the books mentioned at the end of this chapter to try your hand at producing some direct-to-**stereo** recordings. This would help you to understand about mic placement by trying things out and listening to the results, which would be very useful for the ambient recording part of the AS coursework.

Another way of learning more about the recording process is to find a work-experience placement in a small studio. You will not find this easy as there are many health-and-safety issues involved and studios are busy places that often have many applications from

If you can't get into a real studio, try to visit one of these web sites:
http://www.soundonsoundstudios.com/
http://www.multisound.com/
http://www.lydiansound.com/
http://www.mikesounds.co.uk/
http://www.emeraldsound.com/
You can also pick up some tips at this site:
http://www.knowledgehound.com/topics/
   livesoun.htm

hopeful students. If you strike lucky, note that the work will often involve making tea and being sent out for pizzas – but it could also give you the opportunity to watch professionals at work, see how things are set up and pick up tips on various items of equipment.

Above all, listen to the way commercial CDs have been recorded and mixed. Try to be analytical and relate what you hear to what you have read. Listen out for stereo positioning, double tracking, **FX** processors, balance and mixing qualities. Developing a good ear will enable you to learn how other people have succeeded (or failed) in making a good recording and you will be able to apply this knowledge to your own work. Use the successes and mistakes of other people to make your own work flourish.

Time management

You will need to develop your time-management skills in order to get through everything that needs to be handed in by the deadline. Remember that sequences will take much longer to edit than input. Likewise with recordings: don't just assume that the hours you spend in the studio on different takes is all that is needed. You will need to spend time with the musicians preparing for the recording. You'll want to make sure that each player knows their part so that time is not wasted in the studio. You will want to get a feel for the sound of the recordings that you make by spending time checking the acoustics of various rooms and you will probably need to spend many hours producing various trial mixes of the results until you find the one that represents your best efforts.

Remember that you will probably not be able to complete all of your coursework in lesson time, so it's important that you get into the habit of booking the studio or a workstation in your spare time. **Never leave coursework to the last minute. Always prepare.**

Safety

Listening to sounds at the high levels that can be produced by electronic music technology equipment can cause permanent hearing damage. This damage may only become obvious in later life when you find you need a hearing aid earlier than most other people. Your studio should have guidance and operational rules for hearing safety. You only have one pair of ears – protect them.

Further reading

Music Technology: A Survivor's Guide ISBN 1-86074-209-2
Basic Mixing Techniques ISBN: 1-86074-283-1
Creative Recording ISBN: 1-86074-229-7
MIDI for the Technophobe ISBN: 1-86074-193-2

These are all written or edited by Paul White and are part of the *Sound on Sound* series. You could also subscribe to *Sound on Sound* magazine or *The Mix* for updated information on equipment and for tutorials.

For an account of the development of recording technology, try **Good Vibrations** by Mark Cunningham, forewords by Alan Parsons and Brian Eno. *Sanctuary Publishing.* ISBN 1-86074-242-4.

The Development of Music Technology

This area of study runs throughout both the AS and A2 courses. The intention is for you to gain an understanding of the background to music technology. In other words, rather than simply *using* some equipment that happens to be in your studio, you will have some awareness of how that technology has developed and how it has influenced the music that has been made with it.

In the beginning

When archaeologists uncover the remains of ancient civilisations they often discover signs of music-making. It seems clear that people have been making music for thousands of years and that it is fundamental to society. Although humans are equipped with a highly flexible voice, and they can clap their hands to provide percussion, from the earliest times they have used tools to adapt natural objects and materials in order to make new sounds. In that sense music technology has always existed and the music itself has developed alongside the tools used to create it.

Sound is made when air molecules vibrate back and forth, and transmit energy to our ears. Bones within each ear ensure that the sound is funnelled into a tiny and delicate structure, deep in the inner ear, known as the cochlea. This is packed with tiny hairs which react to the **frequency** of the sound and which trigger nerve impulses to the brain. If the frequencies are regular the sound will be perceived as a specific pitch – just as when the eye receives regular vibrations (at a much higher frequency than sound) it sends impulses to the brain which register as a specific colour. More complex patterns of vibrations allow us to distinguish different tone colours, such as the difference between the same note played on a trumpet and a guitar. The strength (or **amplitude**) of the vibrations enables us to differentiate between loud and quiet sounds. We can also perceive the location of a sound because our ears are spaced apart and the brain can decode the slightly different signal received by each ear in order to place a sound within a stereophonic field.

Although there are similarities between the ways the ear and eye work, most humans tend to have much better visual perception than aural awareness. Thus most people can accurately name different colours, but few can identify two different pitches as the notes C♯ and G, even if they recognise that the two notes sound different.

Before the discovery of electricity, all sound had to be generated by some sort of mechanical action on an object in order to vibrate the air molecules surrounding it. This might be:

✦ striking (eg most percussion instruments)
✦ bowing (eg violins and cellos)
✦ plucking (eg harps, guitars and strings played **pizzicato**)
✦ blowing: either directly across the thin edge of a tube (eg flutes) or a reed (eg clarinets or oboes) or by means of vibrating the lips against a mouthpiece (eg brass instruments).

Over the years craftspeople have made an important contribution to improving these basic methods of sound production and technological advances have often led to the creation of new types of music. For example in the 18th century the harpsichord-maker Cristofori invented a new type of keyboard instrument that allowed the player to control the **dynamic** of each individual note. He drew attention to this revolutionary technical advance with the description *col piano e forte* (with quiet and loud) – soon abbreviated to pianoforte or just piano. It enabled composers to write keyboard music with detailed dynamic expression and new styles of music emerged as a result.

When electricity met music

The pace of technological change increased throughout the 19th century, but much more radical developments occured after 1920, as 20th-century life began to depend more and more on electricity. It didn't take long for inventors to discover that certain circuits could **oscillate**, and be used to produce sound. A new breed of electronic instruments emerged, where sound was generated not by mechanical action, but by oscillating electric currents which could be **amplified** and played through a loudspeaker. A famous example of such early instruments was the thérémin (1920) which was played by moving the hands around two antennae. The sound had a pure, ethereal tone, and the instrument looked very futuristic, with the player not even needing to touch it. The thérémin has been used on many recordings, perhaps most famously on the Beach Boys' *Good Vibrations*, and is still occasionally used today.

For an outline of the development of musical instruments through history, leading up to the first electronic instruments, go to: http://music.dartmouth.edu/~wowem/electronmedia/music/eamhistory.html

See http://www.obsolete.com/120_years/ for a marvellous website, dedicated to the huge range of electronic musical instruments that were created in the 20th century. It includes pictures and some sound samples. Look out particularly for the thérémin, the ondes martenot, and the telharmonium.

The ondes martenot (1928) was one of the first electronic keyboard instruments and was used by Messiaen in a number of works, particularly in his *Turangalîla* symphony (1948). The pure amplified sound sails above the orchestra and provides swooping glissandi, courtesy of a mechanism for sliding the pitch continuously.

See http://theatreorgans.com/hammond/ for more on the Hammond organ and Leslie speakers.

The Hammond organ (1933) used toothed wheels spinning in a magnetic field to produce simple electronic waveforms that could be combined to produce more complex tone colours. The amplified signal was often fed through rotating Leslie speakers to give a characteristic sound that was ideal for light-entertainment music in cinemas and theatres. It can also be heard on many pop-music tracks of the 1960s and 1970s.

A history of the electric guitar (and its most famous players) can be found at: http://www.riffinteractive.com/expguitar/ElectricGuitarRoots1.htm

The principle of amplification was also applied to the voice, the use of a microphone allowing a solo singer to be heard above the accompaniment of a big band in the 1930s and 1940s. And, most importantly, it was applied to the guitar (the first commercial electric guitar appeared in 1937) launching not only a new form of solo guitar playing, but also several new streams of popular music.

Synthesisers

Useful information about synthesisers can be found at: http://www.synthzone.com/

Pictures of early synthesisers can be seen at: http://www.synthfool.com/pics.html

Scientists working for RCA in America produced the first music synthesiser in 1955. Based on the still new valve-based computer technology of the day, it occupied an entire room and was programmed by punched paper tape. Ten years later Bob Moog's much smaller transistor-based synthesiser called the MiniMoog became commercially available. By the early 1970s, these portable **monophonic** synthesisers were being used live on stage by bands such as Yes, Genesis and Emerson, Lake and Palmer. Within a decade technology had advanced to allow synthesisers to be **polyphonic** and digital technology led to the development of sequencers and **drum machines**. The musical results were at first robotic, but bands such as Depeche Mode and the Human League used this to signal a new type of music, quite different from live, human performance. Throughout the rest of the century a large number of electronic keyboard instruments and synthesisers were developed, gradually increasing in sonic complexity and reducing in size.

Private study

1. (i) What is meant by the frequency of a sound?
   (ii) What is meant by the amplitude of a sound?

2. List some early electronic musical instruments.

3. How was the thérémin played?

4. What is a polyphonic synthesiser, and when were they first introduced?

For thousands of years the only way to hear a piece of music was to be in the same place as the musicians while they played it. In 1877 Thomas Edison made the world's first sound recording by capturing the vibrations of his voice on a cylinder covered in tin foil. He called this new invention the phonograph. Ten years later the gramophone was developed by Emil Berliner – its adoption of a flat disc instead of a cylinder made it possible to mass-produce recordings by means of a simple stamping process. The gramophone was in wide use by 1910, but the discs, or records, could store only a few minutes of sound and were limited to a very narrow band of frequencies. Special arrangements of classical music had to be made, not only to fit on the disc, but also to ensure that, for example, the lower frequency notes were audible by doubling up bass-parts on a tuba.

Records became truly popular in 1917 with the advent of jazz. This is a good example of how music and technology influence each other. People wanted to hear jazz so they purchased a gramophone – and once the public had the equipment more music could be recorded and sold. The first public radio station opened in the USA in 1920 (followed by the BBC in 1922) and microphone technology was applied to the recording process from 1925.

Two years later the first successful sound film (*The Jazz Singer*, 1927) appeared, with a soundtrack on gramophone records. It was a far less well-known film (*The Air Circus*, 1928) which established the film-sound technology that was to be used for decades to come. This used a technique of recording sound waves as visual images (literally wavy lines) on the film itself, in parallel with the pictures, thus ensuring synchronisation throughout the length of the picture. These waves could be read by optical sensors, amplified and fed to loudspeakers in the cinema. Almost immediately cinemas started to replace live musicians with amplifiers and loudspeakers to meet the demand for this new type of entertainment.

As microphone technology developed, singers could for the first time sing quietly (close to the microphone) and the era of the crooner began, creating superstars of people such as Bing Crosby. Microphones offered an improved frequency range but the quality of sound was still quite low. The shellac records of this era, which rotated 78 times per minute, still had a short play time, and they could often sound scratchy and wobbly in pitch. Sound quality improved dramatically in 1948 with the introduction of **hi-fi** (high fidelity) discs. These long-playing (LP) records were made of vinyl, giving a much better frequency response. They rotated 33.3 times per minute allowing more than 20 minutes of playing time per side.

Recording

For more on the history of sound recording and broadcasting technology take a look at: http://inventors.about.com/library/inventors/blsoundrecording.htm

Read about the Original Dixieland Jazz Band and hear that early recording at: http://www.redhotjazz.com/odjb.html

This was enough to allow a complete substantial work such as a symphony to be released on a single 12-inch disc. Another boom in the industry occurred in the early 1950s with the seven-inch 'single' record, rotating 45 times per minute, helping to facilitate the spread of rock-and-roll.

Stereo recordings were introduced in 1958, and led to a blossoming of the range of microphone techniques, both for making **ambient** recordings and for using **spot-mic** techniques and then **mixing** the final sound.

Tape recording

There was no way of editing early records – if a mistake was made, the recording had to be destroyed and begun again. During the 1930s and 1940s a method of recording sound as magnetic pulses on plastic tape coated in iron oxide was developed from earlier experiments that had used steel wire. As well as providing an alternative to disc-based recording, tape recording introduced the possibility of **editing** the recorded sound. Studios were able to make several takes of a piece on tape and to reduce costs by editing the final recording later, after the performers had left. Tape also provided a method for home users to make their own recordings. Early domestic tape recorders used open-reel tape and were at first expensive. Home recording rapidly gained in popularity and ease of use after the audio cassette, introduced in 1966 for recording speech, was improved sufficiently to be suitable for music.

For further details about musique concrète see: http://www.musespace.com/writings/essays/musique.html

Learn more about Stockhausen at: http://www.stockhausen.org/

Some information about the BBC Radiophonic Workshop can be found at: http://www.glias.org.uk/glias/rws/pgs/a_toc.htm

Boulez became director of the Institut de Recherche et Coordination Acoustique/Musique (IRCAM) in Paris in 1976 – one of the world's leading centres for research into composition, electronic and computer techniques, acoustics and instrument building.

Composers quickly saw that tape offered great potential for creating new sounds by editing existing ones – a process known as **musique concrète.** Tape could be cut and spliced to create a newly-ordered recording. It could be looped, copied and played back at different speeds. These techniques resulted in dramatic transformations of sounds into previously unheard **timbres** and effects. Pioneering work in musique concrète was undertaken as early as 1948 by the French broadcasting authority RTF, which opened a studio for electronic music in 1951. Many of the major composers of the day worked there, including Messiaen and his pupils Boulez and Stockhausen – although the latter soon left to run his own Studio für **Elektronische Musik** in Cologne, Germany, where he could explore the use of electronically-generated sounds and not just tape-based ones. Other early electronic music studios included the BBC Radiophonic Workshop (established in 1958) – its realisation of Ron Grainer's theme music for *Dr Who* (1963) attracted national acclaim.

Private study

1. (i) Who made the first sound recording?
    (ii) Did this use electricity?

2. What was restrictive about recordings in the early 1900s?

3. (i) When were microphones first used?
    (ii) What difference did microphones make to the recording process, and thus to the music?

4. What major differences in recording technology would you notice between a recording from 1920 and one from 1960?

5. What is meant by Elektronische Musik?

Digital technology and computers

Most recording processes before 1980 stored a representation of the sound-waves on moving material (eg tape or disc). This is known as **analogue** recording, since the recorded signal is stored in patterns that are analogous to the waveforms of the original sound. In contrast a **digital** system turns waveforms into streams of numbers. The numbers can be stored, copied and turned back into sound without losing quality. In theory a digital system can perfectly reproduce sound, but much depends on the recording and playback equipment (microphones, amplifiers and loudspeakers).

Digital recording has become increasingly important in the last 20 years. The first popular medium for the distribution of digital audio was the **CD**, first introduced in 1982. Along with **DAT** (1987) and **DVD** (1995) the CD now dominates the music distribution market. A more recent development is MP3, a file format which compresses audio data so that it can be more easily stored and transmitted over the Internet – a mode of distribution that enables musicians to have their work downloaded directly into people's homes.

Digital technology also led to the development of the sampler in the 1980s. This enables short sections of sound to be recorded, edited and manipulated and it quickly gave rise to home-produced recordings and subsequently the dance-music phenomenon.

Since the early 1980s the availability of small, relatively cheap personal computers has transformed the music industry yet again. Computers can be used to record and process sound in the digital domain, and a huge variety of software exists to enable you to:

✦ make **multitrack** audio recordings
✦ control and edit synthesised and sampled sounds
✦ transform sounds
✦ control and edit performance data via MIDI (see below)
✦ print out music notation
✦ send music files around the world on the Internet, or record on to a CD which can be played on any sound system.

However a computer does not need to be a typical desktop device with monitor, keyboard and disk-drives. It can be any machine that works with digital sound; thus synthesisers and effects units can all be considered to be computers.

MIDI

The Musical Instrument Digital Interface (MIDI) was introduced in 1983 as an agreement between manufacturers to allow electronic musical instruments to control each other. It consists of a set of agreed standards for hardware connection, and messages which can be sent from one device to another. MIDI does not send sound data, but rather *control* signals. The major types of message that are sent are based on the sort of features needed for two electronic keyboards to communicate with each other:

✦ note on/off (each time a key is pressed or released)
✦ pitch-bend (based on a pitch-bend lever or wheel)
✦ aftertouch (key-pressure)

Analogue and digital

For an overview of analogue recording see the website: http://arts.ucsc.edu/ems/music/tech_background/TE-19/teces_19.html

Read an illustrated article on the differences between analogue and digital recording at: http://www.howstuffworks.com/analog-digital.htm

Computers and music

For more on music software see: http://www.mtlc.net/main.php

For information about MIDI and audio, see http://www.cakewalk.com/Tips/Desktop.htm

+ program-change (eg selecting a new sound)
+ controller signals (such as sustain on/off, volume level)
+ system messages (used for synchronisation between machines, and more complex communication such as transmitting all of system memory).

More about MIDI can be found in the suggested further reading, and in the section of this guide starting on page 100.

MIDI has become widespread because it provides a very efficient way for one machine to communicate musically with another. Computers can be made to send, receive, store and process MIDI data, and this is the essence of a **sequencer**. Early sequencers had emerged in the late 1970s and at first merely provided a means to loop a series of notes or drum-beats that could be played automatically. Over the years they have developed into complex pieces of software, which allow people to compose and experiment with musical material, by portraying musical data in a number of different representations – graphically, numerically and even as music notation.

 Private study

1. What is meant by analogue recording?

2. What could be done with tape that could not be done with records?

3. Name three types of digital recording media.

4. What types of software are available for music?

5. (i) Does MIDI transmit sound?
   (ii) What are the major types of MIDI message?

6. How does a sampler differ from a synthesiser?

7. How did the first sequencers differ from those we use today?

8. In what ways does the distribution of music by MP3 files offer the potential to change the relationship between musicians and their audiences?

Further reading

The topics outlined in this chapter are covered in much greater detail in **Digital Sound Processing for Music and Multimedia** by Andy Hunt and Ross Kirk. *Focal Press*. ISBN 0-240-51506-4. It has a supporting website with links that will be of general interest and which cover most of the technological concepts in this course: http://www.york.ac.uk/inst/mustech/dspmm.htm – follow the link 'Supporting information for readers' to get to the list of chapters, each of which has its own set of links to sites of interest and further tutorials.

The Studio Musician's Jargonbuster by Godric Wilkie. *Musonix/ Music Sales* (1993). ISBN: 0-9517214-2-9. A glossary of 1500 terms used in music technology and recording.

Music from the Western Classical Tradition

This area of study features in the AS coursework. If you choose the sequencing option one of your two sequences must be of a classical piece, and if you choose recording one of your two recordings must be of a classical piece recorded to two-track. In either case you have to complete a structured commentary about the music.

Let's begin by defining 'classical tradition'. For the purposes of the exam you are not limited to music of the classical period (see below). You can explore anything from the earliest instrumental and vocal music up to the present day, provided that it is art music rather than pop or jazz. You could explore any of the following types of music. Note that the dates given in the margin are approximate – styles of music usually change gradually over many years.

Music of the renaissance, represented by composers such as Lassus and Palestrina, is largely vocal and may not be terribly useful for sequencing. It includes various types of church music, often with smooth **contrapuntal** textures, and madrigals. There is also some instrumental consort music, often featuring the lute.

Baroque music is often extravagant, complex and highly decorated. In terms of sequencing it can be very rewarding as fast movements tend to have tight rhythmic drive and the data is generally fairly easy to input – apart from ornaments (trills, mordents etc) which can be time-consuming if you are not a good keyboard player. Popular instrumental forms of the period include the dance suite, prelude and fugue, sonata and concerto. Some composers worth listening to and studying are Gabrieli, Purcell, Corelli, Vivaldi, Scarlatti, Lully, Couperin, Rameau, Handel and J S Bach.

Classical composers such as Haydn, Mozart and Beethoven were concerned with giving structure to large-scale works by developing musical themes, manipulating harmony to modulate through different keys and using devices such as sonata form to give shape to the music. Popular instrumental forms included the symphony, the concerto, theme and variations and the sonata.

The romantic period saw many composers focusing on fantasy, emotions and literature rather than on form. Instrumental works were often longer and less tightly structured than in the classical era, allowing the composer to express ideas and feelings. The symphony, concerto and sonata were all still popular forms but were extended in length and technical difficulty. Concert overtures were popular and developed into the symphonic poem – a type of **programme music**. Orchestras became much larger during the 19th century, **modulation** to distant keys became common, and harmony became increasingly complex and **chromatic**. Romantic composers include Schubert, Schumann, Mendelssohn, Berlioz, Liszt, Wagner, Verdi, Brahms, Dvořák, Saint-Saëns, Grieg and Tchaikovsky.

As you may have noticed, the time spans of these musical periods have gradually become shorter and this continues to the present day as the communication of ideas speeds up. There were many

It is best to avoid vocal music for sequencing since it is difficult to synthesise effectively and you cannot recreate the all-important words. You will also find that some instrumental timbres work better than others. For instance solo reed and brass voices often sound more realistic than solo strings.

Renaissance 1400–1600

Baroque 1600–1750

A baroque suite consists of a set of short dances such as the minuet, gavotte, bourrée and jig. A fugue is a complex contrapuntal structure based mainly on one or more interlocking themes. A concerto is a piece that contrasts a soloist (or group of soloists) with an orchestra.

Classical 1750–1825

A symphony is a work for orchestra usually in three or more movements. Classical sonatas have a similar structure, but are on a smaller scale (eg for piano or for a solo instrument with piano).

Romantic 1825–1900

An overture in this period is a short, single-movement work for orchestra.

20th and 21st centuries

changes of style in the 20th century, almost decade by decade. Let's take a look at some of the more important ones.

See some of Monet's paintings at: http://webpages.marshall.edu/~smith82/monet.html

Impressionism is a term that was originally applied to painters, such as Monet and Manet, who captured impressions of objects rather than painting realistic detail. Their paintings shimmer with light. The same can be said of much of the music of Debussy and Ravel who often created a soft and dream-like quality in their music. The orchestration and use of harmony particularly helps to convey this feeling of haziness and fluidity in their work.

For more on serialism try (if you dare!): http://www.dpo.uab.edu/~clemmons/458links.html

Serialism was a method of composition developed by Schoenberg and adopted by Berg and Webern among others. The idea was to use each note of the chromatic scale once only in a 12-note series called a note row or tone row. This row can also be used backwards, upside-down (inverted) or both backwards and inverted. In addition it can be transposed to start on any of the other 11 semitones in the octave, giving 48 permutations of pitches in all. Although there is a tight mathematical logic in the way the notes relate to each other, this is not easy to hear and the results sound very discordant – some people feel it is therefore a highly artificial method of composing. You could try using it yourself – it can be fun and is well suited to computer-based composition.

Post-romanticism is the name given to the style of some well-known composers who continued to develop the ideals of the romantic period. They include Mahler, Richard Strauss, Elgar, Puccini and Rachmaninov. These had all started writing in the 19th century, but the influence of romanticism can also be heard in the music of later composers, particularly those writing musicals and film music, such as Gershwin, Bernstein, Lloyd Webber and John Williams.

Neo-classicism was an early 20th-century movement that sought to replace the grand style of romantic music with a purity that evoked the music of earlier ages, often spiced up with modern harmonies and instrumentation. The name again shows how the term 'classical' has more than one meaning, since composers such as Stravinsky, Prokofiev and Shostakovich more often sought their inspiration from baroque music than the classical style itself.

For more on Steve Reich see: http://www.stevereich.com And for Philip Glass go to: http://www.philipglass.com/

Minimalism (or 'systems music' as it is sometimes known) grew out of tape-based experiments in New York in the 1960s. This music is based on the repetition and gradual change of short phrases and can be quite hypnotic. Early minimalism was often electronically manipulated but later works often used small wind, percussion and keyboard ensembles. Riley, Andriesson, Adams, Nyman, Glass and Reich are among the best-known composers in this genre. This style of music lends itself particularly well to computer-based composition and to sequencing.

There are many other types of early 20th-century art music that provide very rewarding listening, including:

✦ folk-influenced works (Vaughan Williams and Bartók)
✦ pieces inspired by popular music (Debussy, Walton, Gershwin and Bernstein)
✦ works that focus on rhythm (Orff, Stravinsky and Holst)
✦ music created from new types of scales and rhythms (Messiaen)

- works that arise from chance elements (Cage)
- electroacoustic music (Stockhausen)
- works in which the performers play a major role in determining the precise nature of the composition (Pendereckí and Berio)
- music-theatre pieces in which the music itself becomes drama (Maxwell Davies and Birtwistle).

And there are major composers such as Britten who don't fall into any of our '-isms' but who drew on whatever sources (including world music) were appropriate for their immediate purpose.

Be aware that some of these musical styles feature techniques that are beyond the practicalities of sequencing. Listen to them by all means, but don't attempt to recreate them as part of your coursework!

Private study

1. Why is 'classical music' a potentially confusing term?

2. Why is it difficult to synthesise vocal music?

3. What types of instrumental sounds tend to work particularly well in sequencing?

4. (i) Why does baroque music often make a good choice for sequencing?
   (ii) What type of music would you expect to find in a baroque suite?

5. (i) Why do you think the range of styles in art music has become much wider in the last 100 years?
   (ii) What types of 20th-century art music do you think might be particularly difficult to sequence?

Here are some websites where you can find out more about music and composers from the western classical tradition:
http://www.classical.net/music/composer/
http://www.music.indiana.edu/music_resources/composer.html
http://www.gprep.pvt.k12.md.us/classical/composers.html
http://w3.rz-berlin.mpg.de/cmp/classmus.html

Choosing a classical piece

If you have opted for recording rather than sequencing, your choice of piece will depend on the repertoire that your chosen performers can offer. It needs to be two to three minutes in length and must come from the western classical tradition. It could, for instance, be a work for solo instrument with piano accompaniment, such as a movement from a sonata. You could decide to work with a much larger ensemble, but you need to consider the practicalities of getting all the musicians together for the recording sessions – it will be very frustrating if key performers are not available when needed. The most important consideration is to use performers who have mastered the music and can present a reliable interpretation of it. You will find it very difficult to concentrate on recording skills if your ensemble is constantly breaking down or having to practise passages during your precious studio time.

If you have opted for sequencing you will have thousands of pieces from which to choose. From our earlier discussion it should be clear that instrumental music is the best choice, especially if it is a piece that features wind (or keyboard) sounds.

The piece you choose must be published in conventional stave notation and should be in no more than eight simultaneous parts. You should work from a full or miniature score, so that you can see the music for each individual part in the ensemble – keyboard arrangements and simplified versions will not give you this degree of detail and are therefore not suitable.

Guidance on a suitable length for the sequence is given in the grid below. You can choose just part of a longer work for sequencing, but it should be a coherent section and you should note that in such cases your structured commentary will need to refer to the entire work or movement – so don't choose anything too long.

The following grid will help you choose a piece for sequencing. The minimum requirement is that your music must:

+ meet **all 11** criteria at level 1 or higher
+ meet **four** of the criteria at level 2 or 3
+ meet **two** of the criteria at level 3.

These are the minimum requirements. It is perfectly acceptable to choose something which meets more of the level 2 and 3 criteria. Note that a keyboard part counts as two parts for exam purposes.

	Level 1	Level 2	Level 3
1	Four independent parts which should include two different instruments	Five or six independent parts which should include two different instruments	Between six and eight independent parts which should include two different instruments
2	No transposing parts	Up to two transposing parts	Three or more transposing parts
3	Treble and bass clefs only	Alto or tenor clef in one part	Alto or tenor clef in more than one part
4	Single time signature throughout (4/4, 3/4, 2/4, 3/8, 6/8, 9/8)	Music in 5/4, 7/4, 5/8, 7/8 throughout	Frequent changes of time signature and/or use of irregular time signatures
5	Key signatures up to two sharps or flats and/or little or no chromaticism	Key signatures up to four sharps or flats and/or some chromaticism	Key signatures up to six sharps or flats and/or a high level of chromaticism
6	No change of tempo	Abrupt change of tempo with no rallentando or accelerando	Flexibility of tempo eg rallentando, accelerando, rubato, pause
7	Little or no dynamic variation	Some general dynamic variation	Dynamic variation applied to individual parts
8	Much repetition and/or doubling	Some repetition and/or doubling in some parts	Little or no repetition and/or doubling
9	16–24 bars	25–32 bars	33–48 bars
10	Simple rhythms and note values	Syncopation and/or triplets	Irregular beat divisions and ornaments
11	Little or no articulation and phrasing	Some consistent articulation and phrasing	Detailed and irregular articulation and phrasing

Things you need to bear in mind when making your choice are:

✦ The end result must be achievable and musically effective. However much you may like, say, Gershwin's *Summertime*, it is unlikely to work well as a sequence – it is vocal music that needs a high degree of rhythmic flexibility and detailed musical expression, and is better suited to live performance.

✦ The piece should show off your skills. If you find some aspects of notation difficult, such as reading unusual clefs or complex key signatures, note that the grid allows you to avoid these, providing you compensate by choosing a piece with different challenges, such as music with frequent changes of time signature and many subtle changes of speed.

✦ You should like the music – after all, you'll be hearing a lot of it in the process of putting it together!

✦ Your teacher is allowed to help you choose and locate the piece – and your teacher may limit your choice, bearing in mind the availability of suitable scores and the variety of work that will need to be covered for the structured commentary.

✦ It is a good idea to choose a piece that is readily available on CD so that you can compare interpretations by others.

✦ It is a good idea to see if there are similar pieces available for practice purposes before starting on the actual coursework. For instance if you choose a gavotte by Bach, there are hundreds of other baroque gavottes available from which to select material for preliminary exercises. Your teacher will be able to give you much more detailed help on such practice material than is allowed for the actual coursework submission, which must of course be your own unaided work. In addition, working with related music will help give you background information that will be useful for the structured commentary.

Make a preliminary choice of several different types of music and then tick-off the boxes on the grid *opposite* to see which meets the minimum criteria for sequencing.

The structured commentary

After your classical sequence or recording has been completed and submitted you will have to complete a structured commentary about the piece and about the interpretation of western classical music. This is done under exam conditions, but you are allowed to use an unmarked copy of the score and either the MIDI file of the sequence or the recording you made, in order to answer the five sections required. For this part of the exam you will be asked about the following four areas – you just need to do the groundwork, prepare yourself thoroughly and write the information down in the 1½ hours allowed.

This includes the form (how the music is put together) and, if you chose an excerpt from a longer piece, how the extract relates to the rest of the movement or work. Make sure that you illustrate your points by reference to specific bars in the score – eg 'the opening

Structure

theme returns in the dominant at bar 14' or 'a short coda starts at bar 40'. Try to show how your awareness of structure has been reflected in the work you submitted. For instance you may have ensured that fragments of an opening theme were highlighted when they reappeared within a complex middle section.

Musical elements

You should mention any important compositional techniques and, if appropriate, write briefly about aspects such as the ways in which keys relate to each other and how chord progressions are used. Remember that the purpose is not to see how much you can memorise about the work – it is to see if you can identify what is important and if you have been able to bring this out in your sequencing or recording. For example the presence of a melody line in the bass or an inner part will probably have influenced your decisions about balance, or the use of a **pedal** and rising **sequence** to generate excitement will doubtless be something that you have tried to reflect in your work. Draw attention to such points, and remember to state where they occur in the score.

In the case of music that has a contrapuntal texture you will probably have attempted to bring out the clarity of the part-writing in your sequence or recording – this is the place to mention it! Similarly you may wish to refer to technical devices such as the use of **hemiola** which you have tried to highlight in your work.

Context

Here you should refer to other related works and to the social, cultural, historical or technological background to the work. Make sure you refer to at least four similarities and four differences between the work you have sequenced and another similar work. Also refer to the circumstances surrounding the composition (was it commissioned for a particular place or group of performers or was it sparked by an event in the composer's life?) and the reasons why you chose the piece (don't say 'my teacher chose it' – that won't pick up a mark!). Again remember that the object is to test your understanding of the music you used, not to see if you can memorise lists of composers or works.

Expression

In this section you should show how the instruments or voices have been used to create specific textures, how the composer has used dynamics and how performers interpret the music through the use of articulation and tempo. You should refer to all of the items concerning expression and explain how you have used technology to capture or recreate them.

Popular Music and Jazz

This area of study underpins all parts of AS Music Technology, and the skills and knowledge you gain will be vital if you go on to take A2, especially in the *Words and Music* option.

First let's attempt some definitions. What exactly *is* popular music? You could say that *all* music is popular because everything is popular with someone! One major factor is that popular music relies heavily on business and commerce, publicity and promotion, chart ratings and awards ceremonies. So there is a definite link between popular music itself, in all of its many forms, and the way it is sold to the public.

Jazz is no easier to define but essentially it is a form of music that developed in America from blues and ragtime, and has a strong element of improvisation. Jazz has at least as many sub-genres as dance music, covering a wide array of styles and line-ups, and we will be looking at a handful of these offshoots and hybrid forms.

Popular music and jazz are not regarded as 'art music' – they are not directly part of the western classical tradition.

Pop styles

There isn't space in this guide to cover every style of popular music but we can look at a few of the more important stylistic developments and the types of music that you are likely to encounter in the exam. Listening to the artists mentioned in the margins is essential to get a feel of the **genres** in order to help you identify them in the exam. Listening to 'Best of …' CDs can be helpful and saves time tracking down individual albums.

AOR

This stands for 'adult-orientated rock' and is alternatively described as 'soft rock' or 'melodic rock'. This guitar-based music has elements of rock music but is generally less hard-hitting often featuring 'power ballads' such as *Everything I do (I do it for you)* by Bryan Adams or Bon Jovi's *Blaze of Glory*. Production is usually polished and slick, with carefully-controlled guitar distortion and fat drum sounds. Lyrical content is inoffensive and usually deals with love – rarely with sex or controversial topics, hence it is suitable for adults who have lost interest in rebellion! This type of music is very radio- and MTV-friendly featuring 4/4 or 12/8 time signatures, catchy **hooks** and emotive singing styles. Popular through the 1970s, 1980s and 1990s.

Blues

Blues has arguably been the most influential genre in the whole of popular music and jazz. Blues developed from the music of black slaves in America into a format comprising chords I, IV and V in either 12- or 16-bar phrases. The subject matter of blues was often melancholic, dealing with the problems and trials of life. The use of **call-and-response** between the vocal and lead instrument (usually guitar) is a prominent feature of much blues.

Here are some sites to keep up with charts and other popular music news:
http://www.dotmusic.com
http://www.musreview.com
http://www.nme.com
http://www.mojo4music.com

This site has a map of different styles of jazz and how they developed:
http://www.acns.nwu.edu/jazz/styles/

Useful books on popular music include **Key Concepts in Popular Music** by Roy Shuker. *Routledge* 1998. ISBN: 0-415-16104-5, and **Rock Music Styles: A History** by Katherine Charlton. *McGraw-Hill* (3rd edition 1998). ISBN: 0-697-34055-4.

Other artists include Foreigner, Michael Bolton, Starship and Whitesnake.

Country blues artists include Blind Willie McTell, Blind Blake and Lightnin' Hopkins.

Country blues, which developed in the country areas of the southern states of the USA in the early 1900s, is characterised by anguished vocals and the use of slide guitar (using a bottleneck). This early form of blues was exclusively acoustic and was often performed by a solo singer accompanying him/herself.

Chicago blues artists include Muddy Waters, Howlin' Wolf, B. B. King and T-Bone Walker.

Chicago blues developed in the city of that name as the African-American population moved to urban areas searching for work and better lifestyle opportunities. The music became electronically amplified and bands featuring bass, drums, harmonica and piano alongside the guitarist were more common than soloists. This gritty and driving sound, often known as rhythm 'n' blues, developed through the 1940s and 1950s and gave birth to rock 'n' roll.

British blues artists include Alexis Korner, Cream, the Yardbirds, the Rolling Stones and Led Zeppelin.

British blues found musicians in the 1960s exploring and popularising the electric Chicago style and blending it with elements of rock music. Initially bands covered American songs but eventually they began to write their own music, which was then popularised in the US by bands such as the Rolling Stones.

Country

Traditional country artists include Hank Williams, Johnny Cash and Willie Nelson.

Country (or 'country and western') has many sub-genres but in general it is music derived from elements of both American folk music (much of which originally came from Europe) and the blues. Traditional country, popular from the 1930s onwards, features slow songs in 4/4 or 3/4. The lyrics are often sentimental and sung with a nasal tone; accompaniment is usually on acoustic guitars.

Bluegrass country artists include the Dixie Chicks and Dolly Parton (listen to her CD *Little Sparrow* to hear the folk roots of country music).

Bluegrass, developed in Kentucky in the 1940s and still prevalent today, is a more upbeat form of country, featuring a picked banjo style, fiddles and mandolins to create a bouncy rhythm. It has a 'barn dance' feel to it. Listen to the Dixie Chicks for superb examples of this style.

Country rock artists include the Eagles and Emmylou Harris.

Country rock was a phenomenon which began in the 1970s and was born of rock artists who were inspired by country music. The music had some traits of soft rock combined with the gentle qualities of country. The Eagles were the epitome of this sub-genre, which lasted through the 1980s.

New country artists include Faith Hill, Reba McIntyre, Billy Ray Cyrus and Shania Twain.

With the huge success of Garth Brooks in the 1990s, country music became more mainstream and started having success in the pop charts. Country began to merge with commercial pop and rock styles and became known as 'new country'. Familiar elements of country are combined with a punchier rhythm section, more use of keyboards, very commercial hooks and production values, and often features dance remixes (hear Lee Ann Womack's various versions of *I Hope You Dance*).

Dance music

This genre has many sub-genres with more appearing all the time. Essentially, dance music (as its name suggests) is primarily for dancing to and the main emphasis is on the beat rather than melodic ideas or lyrical content. While a large amount of popular music has been used for dancing, it is the music which has been made specifically for this purpose that we are referring to.

Disco originated in gay bars in the USA and was made internationally popular by the film *Saturday Night Fever* in 1977. It is characterised by a steady 4/4 bass drum and very lush production values – it was often more the realm of the producer rather than the performer. Arrangements often featured string and horn sections in addition to guitar, bass, drums (or drum machines) and keyboards. Disco was to evolve through Hi-NRG (a faster form of disco) into other forms of dance music.

Disco artists include Village People, Donna Summer, KC and the Sunshine Band, the Bee Gees and Van McCoy.

House music developed through the 1980s, keeping disco's 4/4 beat and adding squelchy, deep bass lines, mechanical, sampled beats and synthesisers. This music was faster than disco and was, more often than not, instrumental. Vocal samples were used but they were often of female singers who either used no words at all or sang phrases such as 'ride on time' which were repeated using the relatively new sampling technology.

House artists include Soul II Soul, KLF, the Shamen and Coldcut.

Techno grew from funk and soul grooves of the 1970s combined with electronic music as produced by Tangerine Dream and Kraftwerk. Its tempo is generally in the range 115–160 **bpm**. Sub-genres of techno are hardcore (where the bpm was raised to very high levels), ambient (where the bpm was lowered and washy synth pads floated over the top) and jungle (related to hardcore but more complex using polyrhythms and fast breakbeats with a dash of dub).

Techno artists include Orbital, Aphex Twin and the Prodigy.

Other forms exist such as:

✦ acid house (characterised by the use of the Roland TB-303)
✦ trance (which uses repeated synth lines in a hypnotic way)
✦ IDM (intelligent dance music)

… as well as happy hardcore, garage and many others. Some are only differentiated by the bpm or the addition of elements such as dub, jazz or ragga to a basic techno setup. You will not need to be familiar with all of the sub-genres of dance music.

Electric folk

A sub-genre of folk music where traditional tunes or modern folk tunes were played by a more rock-based line-up including drums, electric guitars and bass alongside the more traditional fiddles, accordions and acoustic guitars of folk music. This became a popular and commercial style of music in the 1970s.

Electric folk artists and bands include Bob Dylan, Steeleye Span, Fairport Convention and Pentangle.

Glam rock

This genre was an early 1970s phenomenon, which combined structures and rhythmic elements of rock 'n' roll, the distorted guitars of heavy metal and the catchy hooks of pop. It was lightweight music which was often lyrically naive and dealt with rock 'n' roll or teenage issues. As in pop music, songs were short and showed little development – possibly as an antidote to the various kinds of psychedelic rock found at the end of the 1960s. Typical line-ups would include one or two guitars, bass, drums and vocals. Gary Glitter's Glitter Band featured two drummers for a very distinctive sound. Glam rockers wore lamé, sequins, satin platform shoes and make-up, often looking effeminate. To a large extent, the music itself was less significant than the presentation.

Glam rockers include Marc Bolan and T. Rex, David Bowie (listen to *The Rise and Fall of Ziggy Stardust and the Spiders from Mars* for a typical glam CD), the Sweet, Gary Glitter, Elton John and Kiss.

Gospel

Gospel artists include Brother Joe May, Rev. James Cleveland, Mahalia Jackson and the Clara Ward Singers.

Gospel music usually comprises large mixed-voice choirs. The style developed among the black population of the southern states of the USA. It grew from spirituals and blues, and often features a solo singer with the choir working in a call-and-response style. The lead singer often improvised to show technical skill. The sound still has the same flavour as African choral singing (check out Ladysmith Black Mambazo). This music covers the 1930s to the present day where a gospel choir is sometimes used to give a spiritual flavour to rock, pop or dance tracks.

Grunge

Grunge artists include Mudhoney, Stone Temple Pilots, Soundgarden and Nirvana.

Developing in Seattle in the USA, this style features muddy, dark guitar sounds, and is a hybrid of heavy metal and punk. Typically morose or angst-ridden lyrics and dynamics which often build and suddenly cut are features of the genre. This was the most popular heavy rock style of the 1990s.

Heavy metal

Metal bands include Black Sabbath, Deep Purple, Uriah Heep, Megadeth, Motörhead, Metallica, Nine Inch Nails, Marilyn Manson and Tool.

This genre, like dance, has many sub-genres but it is essentially distorted guitar-driven music, which is usually fast and **riff**-based. Emphasis is often placed on the lead guitarist's technical skill and speed (and also the drummer) leading to lengthy solos which demonstrate this skill. Vocals are usually in the upper tenor register and often involve shouting or screaming. Heavy metal, which developed in the late 1960s and carries on to the present day, is largely the province of white teenage males and the music carries a macho quality, leading it to be labelled 'cock rock'. There are very few successful female metal bands. They are sometimes disparagingly labelled 'frock rock'.

Thrash and speed metal are faster versions of heavy metal, still using accomplished technique (often employing 'palm muting' to achieve a distinctive sound), and driving tempos and rhythms. Death metal and black metal took the dark lyrical ideas of thrash and speed to new, disturbing extremes.

Industrial metal uses the sounds of electronic dance music in combination with the distorted guitar sounds of heavy metal and the bleak, dark and angry lyrical content.

Indie

Indie bands to look out for include Blur, Oasis, Pulp, Supergrass and Travis.

This tag originally referred to independent recording companies – small organisations that appeared in the 1980s and 1990s as an alternative to the international corporations that dominate the pop industry. Much indie music was a reaction to synth- and sample-based dance music of the time and often harked back to the music of the 1960s such as the Beatles, the Kinks and the Yardbirds. It is usually guitar-based, featuring jangly sounds and catchy hooks. Britpop was a phenomenon of the late 1980s and early 1990s, which took indie to the mainstream. Inevitably, as indie music became popular it was usually bought-out by major companies and thus lost much of its original independence.

MOR

MOR stands for 'middle of the road' – in other words, music that is completely inoffensive to all. Smooth, mellow arrangements and production coupled with sometimes bland songs and a soft rock or pop feel are characteristic of this genre. Using lush arrangements (often featuring strings), pleasing vocals and love lyrics, this genre, also known as easy listening, was extremely popular in the 1970s.

MOR artists include Barry Manilow, the Carpenters, Dionne Warwick, and Captain and Tenille.

New age

Often referred to as 'crossover', this style of music is a hybrid of classical, minimal and Celtic folk-influenced styles. The aim of the music is to be meditational, spiritual and calming. The roots of new age may lie in the ambient music of Brian Eno, who experimented with music that was 'as ignorable as it was listenable to'. Much new age music uses a combination of washy synths and samples with sound effects (birdsong, whalesong, sea noises etc), traditional instruments and multi-layered vocals. Structure is often less important than texture and 'the vibe'. Some new age artists claim to be able to put the listener into a trance-like state. This music, which developed through the 1990s, has been described as 'yuppie muzak' and is often used as 'wallpaper music' for dinner parties!

New Age artists include Enya, Adiemus, David Van Teighem and Brian Eno.

Prog rock

Growing through the 1970s, progressive rock (sometimes known as art rock) built on classical forms and structures, moving very much away from the three-minute, verse/chorus single format. It often used extended structures and shifting or unusual time signatures to create complex pieces, often using modified sonata forms. Emphasis was placed on clear compositional technique as well as on instrumental virtuosity, and stage shows were as grandiose and as pretentious as the music sometimes was. Extended solos (especially in a live context) were the norm, as were vague and impenetrable lyrics. Queen combined elements of both art rock and glam rock in *A Night at the Opera* (1975).

Prog rock bands include Yes, Genesis, Pink Floyd, Gentle Giant, King Crimson and ELP (Emerson, Lake and Palmer).

Psychedelic rock

Also known as acid rock, this style of music was inspired by drug-related experiences. Emerging in the 1960s, psychedelic rock featured loudness, distortion, strange sounds and bizarre electronic effects to mimic the experience of LSD or marijuana. As with prog rock, pieces were generally lengthy and improvised to a large extent.

Psychedelic rock artists include Pink Floyd, Jimi Hendrix, Cream, Jefferson Airplane and the Grateful Dead.

Punk rock

Punk was a late 1970s reaction to the excesses of progressive rock and the lack of social realism in most pop music of the decade (especially disco). Punk attempted to present raw music, which had nothing more than a few simple chords and high energy levels. There was also increasignly a sense of the reaction to the government of the time and to high unemployment – punk was socially aware and very angry. Much of the intention of punk was to shock, both lyrically and visually. While the music can sound tame today, it still has energy, vitality and gritty realism.

Punk artists include the Sex Pistols, the Buzzcocks, Stiff Little Fingers, the Damned and (to some extent) the Jam.

Hardcore punk took the ethic to an extreme with very fast tempos, shouted lyrics and a sense of amateurism in the performance, production and presentation of albums. Some bands, such as Siouxsie and the Banshees, adopted an 'arty' stance and combined the feel of punk with more complex sounds and structures.

Rap

Rappers include Snoop Doggy Dog, Ice T, Public Enemy, Eminem, MC Hammer and Puff Daddy.

Rapping, or talking rhythmically over music, began in the late 1970s, became popular in the 1980s and continues to the present day. Rap relies on solid rhythmic elements, often sampled, against which to rap the message or political/social commentary. Often known as hip-hop (which is strictly a New York style of rap), it has several sub-genres, including hardcore (dealing with black politics) and gangsta (dealing with violence, drugs and the abuse of women).

There is also a softer form of rap, which has been tailored to include the white market, where the lyrics are less offensive and the beats are more bland and less hard-hitting.

Reggae

This is a general term embracing not only reggae itself but also various earlier forms of Jamaican music including ska, rocksteady and dub. Ska began as an energetic Jamaican interpretation of rhythm and blues into which was woven Afro-Caribbean rhythms and instrumental sounds. This in turn was influenced by soul music to produce the slower, more mellow feel of rocksteady. Huge sound systems were popular in Jamaica and dub grew out of DJs mixing backing tracks with lots of FX and deep, growling basslines.

Other reggae, ska and dub artists include Bob Marley and the Wailers, Toots and the Maytals, Skatalites, Burning Spear and UB40.

Reggae is generally characterised by its choppy offbeats, politically- and socially-aware lyrics (often concerning Rastafarianism) and a sunny, good-time mood. The genre was quite influential on bands such as the Police, Specials and Selector. The last two were known as 'two-tone' as they had band members that were both black and white. Two-tone had a commercial success in the 1980s.

Rock 'n' roll

Rock 'n' rollers include Elvis Presley, Chuck Berry, Buddy Holly, Little Richard, Jerry Lee Lewis, Bill Haley and Gene Vincent.

A style that grew out of rhythm and blues, country music and gospel in the 1950s – and then took over the world! Songs often used only three chords in a 12- or 16-bar blues pattern, were fast, danceable and had catchy hooks. Lyrically, there was a sense of rebellion with the lyrics often referring to rock 'n' roll itself, the freedom of dancing and teenage love (although some lyrics contained slang words for sex, which many people didn't understand). Rock 'n' roll was taken up by white musicians, some of whom kept the vigorous energy of the original form while others sanitised the form to make it less frightening for the moral majority.

The term 'upright bass' is often used in pop and jazz to refer to the double bass, almost always plucked and seldom amplified at this time. Sometimes the weak sound was given percussive accents by plucking the string hard enough to snap back against the fingerboard, hence the term 'snap bass'.

The style featured guitars, upright bass (later replaced by bass guitar), drums, piano and vocals. Many artists used a backing vocal group in a call-and-response manner. Songs were largely in 4/4 and had a **shuffle rhythm**. Rock 'n' roll lasted until the end of the 1960s but continued to have a huge influence on the development of popular music in general through its energy and attitude.

Soul

Developed in the 1960s, soul was the result of rhythm and blues moving into urban centres all over the USA. The music became commercialised, particularly in Detroit, where the Motown label focused on polished pop-soul, often featuring girl groups and lush production. The latter was often by Phil Spector, who pioneered the 'wall of sound' – basically a huge arrangement recorded with gallons of **reverb** and everything very loud!

The vocal style of soul is extremely expressive with high-pitched, emotionally-charged lines and technical improvisation around the melody, demonstrating its links with gospel music. Love was an important lyrical theme and instrumentation sometimes includes string or horn sections as well as the standard band line-up.

Soul brothers and sisters include James Brown, Mary Wells, Wilson Pickett, Aretha Franklin, Roberta Flack, Sam and Dave, and Ben E. King. Some Motown girl groups for you to check out are the Supremes, the Shangri-las and the Ronettes.

Private study

1. What is meant by each of the following terms?
   (i) hook   (ii) call-and-response   (iii) riff.

2. What type of music is bluegrass?

3. How does reggae differ from ska?

4. What are the characteristics of new-age music?

5. How has the blues influenced each of the following styles?
   (i)   Rock 'n' roll
   (ii) Heavy metal
   (iii) Gospel.

Getting to know a good range of pop styles will take time and requires extensive (but enjoyable!) listening. Always try to listen perceptively, noting the techniques, structures and styles used. Ask yourself why a track by, say, Bob Marley sounds different to a song by Jimi Hendrix. Try to identify the influences of earlier styles, such as the blues or heavy metal, in the music you hear.

A useful technique is to tune in at random to a radio station that you don't usually listen to, and to identify what is playing. Look out for stations that specialise in types of pop music that you don't know too well.

Making comparisons can be particularly helpful in this process. Even if you don't have the precise songs listed below, questions of this type can be asked about many different types of music and will help you focus on the musical elements that are important.

1. Compare an early Elvis Presley track with one by Buddy Holly. What are the differences and similarities in these two rock 'n' roll styles?

Note that Elvis, unlike Buddy Holly, did not write music – he was a performer but not a composer.

2. Listen to *Lola* by the Kinks and *Tender* by Blur. Describe how the songwriting of Blur has been influenced by the Kinks.

3. How would you describe *The Adams Family* by MC Hammer and *Stan* by Eminem?

4. What are the key features of the album *The Lamb Lies Down On Broadway* by Genesis that place it firmly in the category of progressive rock?

5. Listen to any track by the Sex Pistols and identify at least three features that are indicative of the punk movement.

Jazz styles

Useful books on jazz include **Jazz Styles: History and Analysis** by Mark C. Gridley. *Prentice Hall*, seventh edition 1999. ISBN: 0-13-021227-X (with CD). **What to Listen for in Jazz** by Barry Kernfeld. *Yale University Press*, 1955. ISBN: 0-300-07259-7 (with CD) and **The New Grove Dictionary of Jazz** edited by Barry Kernfeld. *Macmillan*, 1994. ISBN: 0-333-63231-1 (one-volume edition).

Jazz developed in New Orleans, in the south of the USA, in the early years of the 20th century. Like the blues it spread north to Chicago and then, via gramophone records and radio, soon became known and played around the world. It has had a long period of continual development ever since. Jazz has also had a huge impact on popular music, but it is not itself a type of pop music – indeed, some styles of jazz have been very much a minority interest. In the AS Listening and Analysis paper you will probably not have more than one or two questions on jazz styles.

Dixieland and traditional jazz

The best-known and most influential figure from the days of early jazz is Louis Armstrong. Bands that have revived traditional jazz include those led by Kenny Ball and Chris Barber.

The earliest style of jazz from the 1920s is known as New Orleans jazz or Dixieland. It generally has a swung rhythm in a fast tempo. Bands consisted of a frontline of soloists (eg cornet, clarinet and trombone) who would improvise collectively as well as individually, supported by a rhythm section of upright bass, piano (or banjo) and drums. Tunes were often influenced by ragtime (as exemplified by the work of Scott Joplin) although many other types of music, including the blues, were given a jazz treatment. This early style has been revived several times, notably in the UK in the 1950s and 1960s, and the music of such revivals is known as traditional jazz.

Big-band jazz

Big-band leaders include Duke Ellington, Count Basie and Fletcher Henderson. The dance-band style is typified by Glenn Miller and his Orchestra.

This refers to a style of jazz that emerged in the 1930s and 1940s, using larger ensembles. Typically there would be a horn section of three trumpets and three trombones, a reed section of four saxophones, and a rhythm section of piano, guitar, drums and upright bass. The larger numbers made collective improvisation impractical and so the music had to be arranged and written down, although scores still left room for solo improvising, particularly by the band-leader. The musical style of the period, both in pop music and jazz, is known as 'swing'. It emphasises four equally-weighted beats in the bar, each divided into **swing quavers**. Much big-band jazz was based on the chord patterns (although not the melodies) of popular hits of the day. Many of these patterns, known by jazz players as 'changes', have gone on to form the basis of much jazz improvisation to the present day.

Big bands were also used in the pop music of the period, playing dance music, and accompanying amplified solo singers and close-harmony vocal trios in songs and ballads. Such music was not improvised and is therefore not jazz, although it was influenced by the instrumentation and swing rhythms of jazz. Big bands are still popular today and they do not always play swing – their repertoire may include other types of jazz or arrangements of music from films, stage musicals and so on.

Bebop

Beboppers include Charlie Parker, Dizzy Gillespie, Thelonius Monk and Bud Powell.

Bebop (or simply bop) emerged in the 1940s, partly as a reaction to the increasing commercialisation of swing and partly due to the financial difficulty of maintaining big bands during and after the second world war. Jazz returned to using much smaller ensembles and to focusing once again on solo improvising, often of a most technically demanding kind. Bebop is generally fast and exciting, and often highly discordant – a feature shared with much of the art music of the time. Jazz continued to be based on traditional chord patterns, but these were given complex chromatic alterations. For instance, *Anthropology* by Dizzie Gillespie and Charlie Parker is based on George Gershwin's famous song *I got rhythm* – but the harmony is elaborated almost beyond recognition, and an entirely new theme is substituted for Gershwin's original melody. One element to watch out for is the use of highly syncopated chords, often from the piano, that punctuate a texture of **polyrhythms** so complex that it can be difficult to feel an obvious beat.

Cool jazz

Starting around 1949 and evolving over the next 25 years, 'cool' ironed-out some of the more jarring elements of bebop, particularly the dissonances that were so freely used. It is often very mellow, with a laid-back beat (quite different to the frantic pace of bebop) and an emphasis on understatement. Unusual metres sometimes appeared (as in the 5/4 time of Brubeck's famous *Take Five*), along with instruments rarely used in jazz before, such as the flute and vibraphone. Ensembles were often no more than trios or quartets. Some of the jazz from this period led to the easy-listening music called 'lounge' that you can still hear in lifts and hotel restaurants.

Cool artists include Miles Davis, Lester Young, Chet Baker and Dave Brubeck (although some of Brubeck's work is termed 'third stream' because of its combination of jazz with classical music).

Avant-garde jazz

First appearing in the 1960s (when it was often called free jazz) avant-garde jazz emphasises melodic invention. Unaccompanied playing is an important part of the style, allowing players to break free of a regular pulse and set chord sequences. The style, which continues to the present day, pushes jazz to new frontiers in terms of flexibility and experimentation, and can sometimes seem chaotic in its free approach to rhythm and tonality.

Avant-garde is a French expression meaning 'ahead of the front'. It refers to composers and other artists who use techniques which are perceived to be breaking new ground. Avant-garde jazz artists include Miles Davis, Ornette Coleman, John Coltrane and Sun Ra.

Fusion

Fusion, as the name implies, is a blend of styles. As rock music became more complex in the 1970s, it was mixed with jazz, taking the most interesting elements of both genres, particularly unusual or changing time signatures and the creation of new textures using keyboards and FX. The 1980s saw the decline of complexity in rock music and a similar decline in fusion, which became softer, more mellow and more focused on production values and melodic interest as improvisation took more of a back seat. This new, more easy-listening style is sometimes referred to as pop jazz or smooth jazz.

Fusion artists include Weather Report, Pat Metheny and Return to Forever.

Vocal jazz

This simply refers to jazz of any period in which a vocalist takes prominence rather than instruments. A common technique is a jazz singing style called scat in which the vocalist improvises a melody to nonsense syllables, sometimes in a very fast and brilliant style. Also typical are the liberties singers take with the original melody, bending and reshaping it to suit their own personal style.

You can hear an early example of slow scat singing in Louis Armstrong's *West End Blues* (in the Edexcel *New Anthology of Music*). Jazz singers include Ella Fitzgerald, Cleo Laine, Mel Tormé, Sarah Vaughan, Frank Sinatra, Bobby McFerrin and the jazz vocal group Manhattan Transfer.

Private study

1. What instruments might you expect to hear in (i) the frontline and (ii) the rhythm section of traditional jazz?

2. What instrument(s) would you expect to hear in a big band of the swing era that you would not normally hear in a New Orleans jazz band?

3. What do jazz players mean by 'the changes'?

4. Explain the meaning of the term 'swing quavers'.

5. What are the main features of bebop?

Jazz FM broadcasts in London, some other parts of the country and via the internet. See http://www.jazzfm.co.uk/

BBC Radio 3 regularly broadcasts jazz. See http://www.bbc.co.uk/radio3/jazz/

http://www.notz.com/ukjazz.htm carries news about jazz in the UK, including jazz festivals and links to other jazz sites.

For national listings of jazz gigs, news and information about jazz in education go to http://www.jazzservices.org.uk/

As with pop music, try to include a good range of jazz styles in your listening. In some parts of Britain there are jazz radio stations and most large record stores will have a jazz department. But in order really to understand the spontaneity of jazz, it is much better to see a band playing live rather than just listening to CDs. Most larger towns have a pub or arts centre where bands play, or failing that there are many commercially-available videos of well-known jazz artists. Once again, comparing different recordings is a good way of getting to know the music in depth. Here are some suggestions for you to use or adapt:

1. Compare recordings of *Mack The Knife* by Ella Fitzgerald and Frank Sinatra. How does the treatment of the vocal line differ?

2. What different types of jazz (and related genres) do Manhattan Transfer use on their album *Extensions*?

3. Compare the big bands of Count Basie and Glenn Miller. How do the two bandleaders approach the medium of jazz?

Arranging The knowledge you gain about pop and jazz will help you think creatively about arranging. How can you change music from one style into another? Which elements would you keep and which would you modify? See if you can imagine the following:

+ *Judy Teen* by Cockney Rebel treated as a punk song
+ *Pinball Wizard* by the Who reworked as a techno track
+ *Take Five* by Dave Brubeck played in 4/4 time
+ *Taxman* by the Beatles reworked in ska style
+ *Common People* by Pulp interpreted as an acoustic guitar ballad
+ *Let's Dance* by David Bowie reworked as a grunge experience
+ *America* by Simon and Garfunkel treated as prog rock.

All of these are possible. What would you need to change? What are the possibilities and the limitations? Which would be the most and the least effective? How would the new arrangements enhance, enliven or add to the original version?

Listening and analysing Once you get to know the music itself (not just its description), you should be able to identify styles with ease. Listen for structures, lyrical content, instrumental combinations and playing styles to recognise genres and time-scales. Beware of new recordings of old songs. You may occasionally be asked about the period of the *song* rather than of the *recording*. They may not always be the same.

Sequencing

AS requirements

For AS music technology you must choose **either** sequencing **or** recording. We discuss recording on page 42.

If you choose sequencing you are required to produce:

+ a sequenced performance of a piece from the western classical tradition that faithfully follows a chosen score

+ a contrasting sequenced performance that can come from any musical idiom – but note that your sequence must **faithfully follow a full score** for this piece as well

+ a log for each sequence that lists the equipment used and explains your decisions about the shaping of the music.

You will also have to complete a structured commentary about the piece from the western classical tradition, as explained on page 23.

Note that you may not use your own compositions as a basis for sequencing in this component.

Each sequence must be submitted on CD or mini-disc, along with the scores and logs.

The sequencing option accounts for 40% of the total AS mark (30% for the sequences and 10% for the structured commentary).

A2 requirements

At A2 sequencing, recording and producing skills are combined in a single component, which we discuss on page 81.

What is sequencing?

Each time a piece of music is performed by human players the result is unique. Music notation shows the composer's intentions, but it is only a guide, and aspects such as tempo, dynamics and the modification of note-lengths to phrase and articulate the music, are interpreted differently in every performance. Such performance information is sent and received by MIDI devices as numeric data. This includes which notes are pressed, which sounds are selected, how other controls (such as pitch-bend and aftertouch) are used, and which settings are used for parameters such as volume, panning, sustain pedal, reverb and other effects. These numbers can be captured, stored, inspected, manipulated and replayed as a musical performance when sequencing. For more technical detail about MIDI you may wish to refer to the A2 section on Controlling and Interpreting MIDI Data (starting on page 100) as you work through this chapter.

These days sequencing is normally carried out on a computer, loaded with software designed for the task. A computer allows the data to be displayed in a variety of ways (including graphically) and it offers various tools to simplify editing, including the mouse. It also enables the data to be stored on disk for future use.

Getting started

The most common method for entering notes into a sequencer is by playing them on an external MIDI keyboard. For recording, the MIDI OUT of the keyboard should be connected to the MIDI IN of the computer. You will probably use the computer's soundcard to play back the recording, listening over headphones. If you want to play it back through the keyboard, the computer's MIDI OUT will need to be connected to the MIDI IN of the keyboard. More complex systems may have many other connections – audio leads to studio monitors, effects units, recorders and so on. Make sure you know how to set up equipment correctly and safely. Other users may not leave it as you left it and it is easy to become confused (and cross!) when you don't hear something you are expecting.

Look around your studio and check what each piece of equipment does. Think about how you might use each item in your work. Familiarise yourself with your sequencer. You may well have to look in the user guide, helpfile or other documentation to discover how to carry out particular operations. Sequencing is a practical subject and there are many aspects to learn. The best way to master it is through plenty of practice on the sequencer that you will be using to create your music.

A sequencer is organised rather like a tape recorder with a number of **tracks**. There are usually at least 16 and each can be used to record the MIDI data for a different instrument in the piece. Notes are best entered in **real time** against a metronome click, which can be set (usually in bpm) to the speed required. Remember also to set the number of beats per bar before you start, by entering the **time signature** of the piece. If you find real time difficult, you can slow the speed down to something more comfortable but remember that this may affect things like staccato notes, which will probably sound far too short when replayed at the right speed. The metronome click can also be set to provide a *count in* of one or more bars (the sequencer becomes your virtual conductor) so that you know at what speed to play and when to start.

Sequencers also allow you to use **step time** input or to enter notes by simply clicking them into place on an editing screen. This means you can proceed as slowly as you want – you can even make a cup of tea between notes! But it is best to avoid this if you can, as note starts and velocities will be boringly uniform and they will require a vast amount of editing in order to achieve acceptable results.

The main controls on a sequencer are usually laid out like those on a tape recorder (see *left*). The 'song pointer' acts like a tape counter, showing the current location expressed in bars, beats and fractions of a beat (ticks). To make a recording, select MIDI track 1 and click record. You should hear the metronome and after the count in you can start playing something (anything you like!) on the keyboard. When you have finished, click the stop button. To hear your recording, click rewind to set the recording to the start, and then click play. Before going on, try recording a tune that doesn't begin on the first beat of a bar – something like 'Happy birthday to you', that starts on the third beat of the bar in 3/4 time. Note carefully how your sequencer deals with this and how it counts the bar numbers in cases like this.

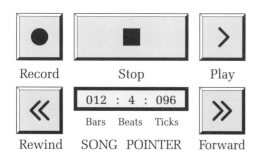

Record   Stop   Play

012 : 4 : 096

Bars   Beats   Ticks

Rewind   SONG POINTER   Forward

Recording modes

Overdub and replace

When new MIDI data is added to a track, as in the example above, the sequencer is working in record (or **overdub**) mode. When existing MIDI data needs to be replaced, the sequencer has to be switched to overwrite mode (or replace mode).

Punch in

If you make a mistake you may need to replace only a part of your recording. This can be done by setting **punch-in** and **punch-out** points using *locators* to specify precise bar and beat numbers. Set the locators to the start and end points of the section to be replaced. Rewind to a convenient place and press record. The sequencer will start off in play mode so you can hear what has been recorded, but when it reaches the punch-in location it will start recording so that you can play the correct version. When it reaches the punch-out location, it will change back to play mode. Your sequencer should have an *undo* function that will enable you to revert to the original recording if the punch-in was not to your liking.

It is usually possible when playing live to build up a sequence in steps by repeating a section over and over again in overdub mode, adding a new layer of notes each time round. This is known as *cycling* or *looping*, and the start and stop positions are again set using the locators. This can be a very useful way of building up a drum pattern layer by layer.

Cycle mode

Editing a sequence

Unless you are a brilliant keyboard player you should expect to spend a lot of time editing and refining your work. This needs a critical ear and clear thought about what you are trying to achieve. Here are some of the techniques you will need to master.

Sequencers provide various **quantise** options for adjusting groups of notes. **Note-on** quantise will nudge notes to the nearest beat or sub-division of a beat. The amount of shift is set with a quantise value – for instance, if you choose a crotchet (quarter-note) value for a piece in 4/4 time, all notes will shift to the nearest beat (1, 2, 3 or 4) in the bar. A large value like this can wreak havoc with shorter notes. In the example *right* the first four notes have been correctly shifted on to the starts of beats – but so has the fifth, which is almost certainly wrong. There are two rules for successful quantisation:

✦ the quantise value must not be greater than the shortest note value in the music being edited

✦ notes in your original recording must not be out of time by more than 50% of the quantise value.

It is therefore wise to choose low quantise values and to realise that quantisation will not be able to correct very inaccurate playing. You also need to be careful if the beats include irregular note-groups such as triplets or swing quavers. These can be wrecked by the wrong quantise value. If you need to quantise such sections, look for a 'swing' or 'triplet' setting that you can apply to just these parts.

Quantising can also usually be applied to note-lengths (to even up their lengths) and to velocities (to give them all the same loudness). Strict quantisation is a feature of some types of synthesised dance music, but it is best avoided in other genres since many aspects of musical performance can be lost. More intelligent quantise options, such as a percentage shift, are often available and these can produce results that are closer to a human performance of the music.

Sequencers offer a variety of views on the data they store. For editing individual notes the most useful is that provided by the **piano-roll** display, sometimes called the key editor or grid editor. This shows notes in the form of a graph, like the examples in the margin above. Each note can be selected with the mouse and then deleted, copied to the clipboard (a temporary memory location in the computer)

Remember to back up your files, especially when editing. Copy a track before editing it, so that you can compare the edit with the original and start again if necessary.

Quantising

Notes as played:

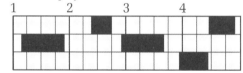

Notes after quantisation to quarters:

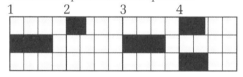

Remember that most styles of music depend on subtle variations of note lengths and volume to sound interesting, as well as on notes that are pushed fractionally before the beat to create tension or fractionally after to create relaxation. Ill-judged quantisation can easily remove these qualities.

Note editing

Bar/Beat	Event	Value	Velocity	Length
1:01:012	Note	F 4	113	121
1:02:006	Note	E 4	106	143
1:03:015	Note	D♯4	88	132
1:04:000	Note	E 4	97	119

for pasting elsewhere, changed in pitch by moving it vertically, shifted in time by moving it horizontally, shortened or lengthened by dragging one end or have its velocity changed. Groups of notes can be selected (usually by 'rubber banding' an area with the mouse or by holding down the shift key while clicking on the notes) – any editing functions will then be applied to them all. This is particularly useful if you want to **transpose** a section, perhaps for copying and pasting elsewhere in the piece.

In a list editor each of the individual MIDI events is displayed in numeric rather than graphic form. The parameters associated with each MIDI event are shown and where appropriate, they can be edited by typing in new values. Alternatively the mouse can often be used to increase (right button) or decrease (left button) the values. Each MIDI event has a start time associated with it and a note event will have its pitch, length and velocity indicated.

Many sequencers can produce a score from the recorded MIDI data, and this too can be edited. When raw performance data is initially transformed into a score the results can look hopelessly confusing (see the example on page 68). To produce decent-looking notation the sequencer will need to apply quite different quantisation to that suitable for performance data. Some sequencers will make these adjustments to the score only – and any editing you do, such as changing the pitch or length of notes, may be applied only to the notation and will have no effect on the sound. Others will apply changes to the MIDI data itself, and this may introduce unwanted alterations to the quantisation of the sound of your work.

Score editing must therefore be used with caution. It can work well when used in parallel with another form of editing, but it is difficult to use successfully on its own. If you are considering using a score editing facility for your sequence, check very carefully first that it does what you want and, if necessary, keep separate versions of your files for performance and notation.

Editing controller data

All aspects of the MIDI data can be manipulated from the sequencer. MIDI controller information, such as modulation wheel settings (controller 1), volume (controller 7), stereo panning (controller 10), sustain pedal (controller 64) and effects such as reverb (controller 91) can be changed or added to the sequence where you feel they enhance the final performance. Program changes can be made if you want to change the sounds used on a track. Pitch-bend can be applied to any note where you feel it provides a more musical result. Further familiarity with your particular sequencer is needed to find out how to change these MIDI performance parameters. You will find many are available in the piano-roll or list editors and some are available within their own menus. There is no substitute for trying them out and listening to the results that are possible.

Tempo changes

During editing you will probably need not only to finalise the overall speed of the sequence but also to make subtle changes to enhance the performance. Tempo rarely remains static, unless the style demands a particularly robotic approach, and you will need to give attention to such matters as fractionally moving the speed on towards a climax, or easing it back by a few bpm at points of relaxation (think of the job of a conductor in orchestral music).

Tempo (and time signature) changes can usually be varied at any position using a special conductor or master track. You may also need to see how your sequencer copes with a pause – sometimes this can be achieved by briefly setting the tempo much slower, sometimes it will need an extra beat added which may necessitate, say, a bar in $\frac{5}{4}$ time – and often both methods are needed.

Working with many parts

In order that a different type of sound can be played by each part, there are 16 MIDI channels available. By default sequencers set track 1 to MIDI channel 1, track 2 to channel 2 and so on. If your music requires say a flute, oboe and bassoon the notes for each should be recorded on separate tracks (each with its unique MIDI channel number), and the patches for each should be set for the required instrument. You have to ensure that the appropriate MIDI channel is set on the synthesiser(s) used for playback of each track.

MIDI channel 10 is widely used for the drum track. It is good practice to keep to this convention since most synthesisers have a drum kit assigned to MIDI channel 10 by default. You record a drum track in the same way as for any other instrument, perhaps at a slower speed. Different pitches on the keyboard are mapped to specific drum sounds (snare, cymbal etc). Drum tracks are often quantised to achieve clear regular beats. Sort out which notes produce the drum kit items you require. Editing can be carried out in the same way as for other tracks, although some sequencers have special drum-track editing facilities.

A drum map allows individual instruments within the kit to be reassigned to different pitches, but this should be left at the default General MIDI setting to ensure that your work sounds as you intend when played on other GM equipment.

Achieving a musical result

When you make a sequence, you are in charge of everything, both musical and technical. Making a musical sequence for submission to the examiners is rather like serving them a good meal. It is important that only the best ingredients are used along with the most appropriate processing techniques. Listeners have certain expectations of what they are hearing which will be triggered by the instruments, time signature, tempo and patterns of the music. Decide how you want to realise your musical ideas and then find out how to achieve it with your sequencer. Don't simply use some feature of the sequencer just because it is available, and merely hope for the best in terms of a musical result.

Instrumental realism

If your music is intended to emulate the sounds of orchestral or other acoustic instruments, it is essential that you bear in mind what is and is not possible to play on them, and that you listen critically to their synthesised counterparts. Be aware in particular of their playing ranges and basic playing issues that determine phrasing such as breathing and bowing. When sequencing a drum kit or keyboard parts, remember that drummers only have two hands and keyboard players only have ten fingers (although pipe organists also have two feet on the pedalboard for bass notes). Guitarists cannot play chords containing more notes than there are strings on the instrument! Keyboard players can only play chords containing notes within reach of their two hands! Wind players cannot produce overlapping notes even when playing legato.

Dynamics and accents should always be adjusted by using velocity levels, not the volume controller. The volume control is more like a fader for bringing instruments in and out of the mix, and will not produce convincing dynamic variations.

Work out phrasing that is musically appropriate and also likely to be possible in a single breath or in one bow movement for the instrument concerned. Mark up a copy of the score appropriately and ensure you follow this in your recording. Expect to spend a lot of time adjusting velocity levels and lengths of individual notes so that the music sounds well phrased and musically articulated.

Remember that you may need to spend time practising each part before recording it. Listen critically during your practice and live performance in order to achieve the best result for each part before proceeding to the next. If you decide to play the notes slowly using the metronome click track and perhaps some overdubbing, remember that fast passages whose rhythms are left to the performer, such as trills and cadenzas, must be slowed down also, otherwise they will sound wrong when speeded up. The musical quality of your overall sequence (on which you will be assessed) can only be as good as the individual musical raw material you put into it.

Instrumental sounds

Get to know the sounds available to you and note the program numbers of sounds you like and why. Develop a vocabulary for describing sounds (you will need to do this in your log). Use words like bright, dull, warm, cold, lifeless, rich, pure and thick.

Get to know the sounds that are available on your synthesiser, listen critically and choose carefully. Be aware that none are fully realistic over the full pitch and dynamic range of their acoustic counterparts. Orchestral strings are the hardest to sequence convincingly, mainly because synthesisers do not provide the degree of control that is available to the string player, and because the real-life sound is made up from many individual instruments. The sequenced result for orchestral strings can be improved by making multiple copies (using the copy and paste functions) of each string part and then adding different small (and that means small) amounts of pitch-bend and volume difference to each copy. Listen carefully to the attack of the sounds available – a slow-speaking brass voice may not work well on a fast-moving trumpet part, and you may need to edit the sound's **envelope** or choose a different brass sound. Don't forget that particular notes may need special treatment, such as some extra modulation to warm a climactic high note.

Mixdown

Once all the parts are recorded you become the musical director, shaping the data to achieve the performance you intend. The overall tempo should be set by listening rather than relying entirely on the score – for example you might feel that 63bpm produces a more musical result than the indicated ♩=60. Set the balance between instruments using the volume controller for each track. If the piece is intended to emulate an acoustic performance, the overall balance should not change during the course of the piece. Try to monitor the mix on decent loudspeakers and not just on headphones.

Remember to make a note in your log of any such choices and your reasons for making them.

Consider how you want each instrument to appear on the 'sound stage'. The sounds of any musical group are spread out in space and this is not only related to the left-right dimension which you can control with stereo panning, but also the front-back or depth aspect. You have some control over the latter through the subtle use of reverb and volume on each individual part (that's *subtle* in both cases!). The further away a sound source is in a space, the greater the reverb and the less the volume on that sound when it reaches the ears of the listener.

Your final submission

Before completing the work it is worth seeking a second opinion and critical comments from someone. It is easy to hear the piece as you expect it to sound rather than what it actually sounds like simply because you are so close to the detail. Be aware also of ear fatigue where your critical listening faculty becomes tired from listening for too long or at levels that are too high.

Before saving the final version of the MIDI file, ensure that your tracks are labelled clearly, perhaps with the instrumental part names (eg piano, guitar, trumpet, drums). These names should also be used in your sequencing log also to make it easy for the examiner to see the tracks to which you refer. Choose appropriate filenames for your pieces ('minuet2.mid' looks much better than 'file134298'). Lastly, delete any tracks that are not part of the final sequence unless these form an important part of the development process of your sequence (detailed in your log).

When making the audio recording of your sequence, it is important to set levels high enough to get a good signal but not so high that distortion arises. Check that the recording is free from clicks, distortion and the hiss of high-frequency noise that can easily be present in some computer-based systems – many sequences are spoilt by rushing or carelessness at this final stage.

Make sure your floppy disk and CD or mini-disc are clearly labelled with your name, candidate and centre number, exam year and the titles of your pieces. Floppy disks and mini-discs should be write protected and CDs properly closed – try to check them both in a different computer, by opening all of the files on them, so that you can be sure all is well.

What the examiners look for

For a really good mark the examiners will be looking for evidence of the following in your work:

+ a high degree of technical and expressive control
+ full use of articulation, dynamic range, balance and timbre
+ a musical and accomplished performance
+ a stylistic interpretation
+ above all, accuracy in pitch and rhythm.

Further reading

Sound on Sound and *Computer Music* magazines are good sources for sequencing hints and tips. Both are available online:

http://www.sospubs.co.uk and http://www.computermusic.co.uk

The 'in sequence' series of books by Paul Terry and William Lloyd (published by *Music Sales*) gives many practical tips, exercises and detailed scores of complete pieces for sequencing:

Music in Sequence, ISBN: 0-9517214-0-2
Classics in Sequence, ISBN: 0-9517214-1-0
Rock in Sequence, ISBN: 0-9517214-5-3.

Recording

AS requirements

For AS Music Technology you must choose **either** sequencing **or** recording. We discuss sequencing on page 35.

If you choose recording, you are required to produce:

✦ a recording of a piece from the western classical tradition, using ambient-mic technique and recording direct to stereo

✦ a recording of a piece in any genre, initially made on between four and eight tracks, using close-mic techniques (and/or DI) and overdubbing, that is then mixed down to a two-track stereo

✦ a log for each recording that lists the equipment employed and explains your decisions about how it was used.

You will also have to complete a structured commentary about your chosen classical piece, as explained on page 23.

Note that you may not record your own compositions for this component and that the recordings must be digital.

Each recording should be two to three minutes in length and must be submitted on CD or mini-disc, along with the logs. You are allowed to retake the recordings as many times as practical within the time available, but the work must be done under the supervision of your teacher, and must not be done in a commercial studio.

The recording option accounts for 40% of the total AS mark (30% for the recordings, and 10% for the structured commentary).

A2 requirements

At A2 sequencing, recording and producing skills are combined in a single component, which we discuss on page 81.

Introduction

This area of study is concerned with the recording process, which involves the capture, manipulation and reproduction of sound. Capturing your sound requires the application of microphone techniques, an understanding of your sound sources and the venues in which they are recorded. Manipulation requires you to route your audio signals through a mixer to and from a multitrack recorder using effects processors if required. Reproduction is where your recorded sounds are mixed and further manipulated for playback and storage on a stereo recording medium such as CD or mini-disc.

Learning recording techniques is very similar to learning how to play a musical instrument. Practice is vital if you are to master the equipment itself so that you can move to the more interesting and demanding task of using it to give form to your musical ideas. Furthermore, although the following sections discuss tried-and-tested working methods, there are no hard and fast rules in recording. Experiment where you can, time permitting, and if you get a result that sounds good for what you are trying to do, then go with *your* method rather than how you think it should be done.

Two-track stereo recording

The first point to consider is the piece you wish to record and this will depend on the performers you can call upon and the time you have available. An ideal scenario for this assignment would be a soloist with piano accompaniment. This allows you to experiment with your recording techniques to get a good result, without being too complex as a sound source or as difficult as a large group of performers to manage and organise.

It will make your task very much easier if you can work with reliable musicians who know the music well – you will not want your studio time eaten away by unprepared performers who have not practised their parts, or who forget to bring their music. Equally, you yourself will need to be well-prepared – don't spend half the time trying to locate equipment and understand how it works. Make sure everything is set-up before the start of the session, check that music stands and seats are suitable, and that the lighting is adequate. Allow plenty of time for the session – at least two hours for your two-track recording.

Venue

In the western classical tradition the selection and use of an appropriate venue for music is highly important. The venue imparts a particular acoustic characteristic on any sound heard within it so if possible you should aim to choose a room or hall that has good acoustic properties. Of particular importance is the level of background noise and the amount of reverberation present. Background noise (for instance a car going past outside) can ruin an otherwise perfect take. Too much reverberation will mean your recording lacks clarity; too little and it will sound dead and lifeless. Both extremes will also make it difficult for your musicians to give of their best. In general try to record in an auditorium designed for the live performance of music, or perhaps a church, rather than a rehearsal room or general-purpose hall. Visit your potential venue prior to your scheduled sessions and do a simple analysis by asking yourself these questions:

✦ Can I hear any outside noise?
✦ Is the hall close to a road, under an airport flight-path or similar potential noise source?
✦ How well isolated is the room? How good is it at rejecting noises from outside? If in a school, is it possible to avoid noise from pupils, school bells etc at the time of the recording session?
✦ Is there noise inside the room? Water pipes? Air conditioning?
✦ If I clap my hands, how long does the reverberant sound last?
✦ Are there any noticeable and maybe troublesome echoes?
✦ Are there curtains or drapes on the walls that I might be able to use to cut out noise and reduce the level of reverberation?
✦ Where can I put the performers? Will they have enough space and light?
✦ Where are the mains sockets? Are there enough of them for my needs?
✦ Where can I put my recording equipment and microphones?
✦ Can I get the equipment close enough to the performers without being in their way, or alternatively is there a suitable separate area that I could use as a control room?

Microphones

The next task is to select the microphones you will use to record your performers. There are many types available, although they can be classified by their design and associated properties.

Microphones contain a diaphragm that moves backwards and forwards according to the sound waves that hit it. These movements are converted into an electrical signal. In a **dynamic microphone** the diaphragm is attached to a coil of wire suspended in a magnetic field. As it moves an electrical signal is generated analogous to the original sound wave.

If the condenser mic is not an **electret** type, additional electronics are required in the microphone housing to charge the plates of the capacitor. Even if it is, there will be a preamp in the mic to boost the signal. This additional circuitry means that condenser mics have to be powered – either via an internal battery or more commonly by **phantom power** supplied from the mixing desk to which they are connected.

Find out about the characteristics of specific microphones at:
http://www.akg-acoustics.com/
http://www.shure.com/

The diaphragm in a **condenser microphone** is designed to be conductive and has another fixed plate spaced closely behind it separated by a layer of conductive insulation. These two plates are charged with static electricity forming a capacitor (hence the alternative name of capacitor microphone). As the diaphragm moves, the distance between the plates is varied, changing the capacitance and again resulting in an electrical signal analogous to the original sound wave.

Dynamic microphones are quite robust compared to the delicate circuitry and operation of condenser mics. They are commonly used for live pop music as they can withstand nightly use on tour in public venues, without concern for the reliability of their operation. Condenser microphones are more generally used for studio work or for classical recording, although dynamic microphones are also desirable in some studio applications. The qualities and features of the two types can be summarised as follows:

Condenser microphones

✦ wide, extended and generally more linear frequency response
✦ detailed, clear sound with good high-frequency pickup
✦ sensitive with good transient response
✦ require battery or external phantom powering
✦ delicate construction implies they must be treated with care
✦ high output level means less gain required at mixer input and so they often generate less noise (hiss).

Dynamic microphones

✦ rougher frequency response (but this can be desirable in some contexts)
✦ good for high volume levels
✦ poor transient response
✦ robust and reliable, withstanding heat, cold and humidity
✦ generally low output level requires high gain level at mixer input
✦ low level of performer handling noise.

Pickup patterns

Microphones are also classified according to their polar pickup pattern or how sensitive they are to sounds arriving from different directions. There are five pickup patterns in common use, which are shown here as viewed from above the microphone:

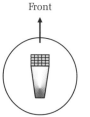 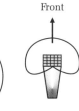  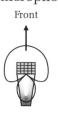 

| Omni-directional | Cardioid | Supercardioid | Hypercardioid | Figure of eight |

Omnidirectional microphones:

✦ exhibit a wide, flat, extended frequency response
✦ give good pickup of both low and high frequencies
✦ will pickup a lot of room reverberation
✦ offer poor isolation unless close to the sound source
✦ are not affected by **proximity effect**.

Microphones in the cardioid family:

✦ reject reverberation, background noise and spill
✦ offer effective isolation
✦ are good for stereo coincident or near-coincident miking
✦ exhibit the proximity effect in relative level of bass frequencies.

The cardioid has the widest front angle pickup and best rear rejection. Supercardioid has more isolation and will pick up less reverberation. Hypercardioid has the most side rejection, the most isolation and the most rejection in terms of reverb, spill and background noise.

Microphones with a figure-of-eight response:

✦ have good front and rear pickup, with maximum rejection of sounds arriving from the sides.

For your classical recording two identical *condenser* microphones will be required due to their good frequency response, clear output, sensitivity and low noise. The pickup pattern you use will depend on how you place your microphones in relation to the sound source and the venue. In general a standard cardioid pattern will produce good results for most applications.

Microphone positioning

When you carry out a recording of this nature you are effectively attempting to recreate for the listener the actual experience of being in the venue sitting in front of the ensemble you are working with. The success (or otherwise) of this often comes down to the careful positioning of your selected microphones to achieve the best result. Mic placement allows you to control the sense of distance of the ensemble, the balance between the instruments and the stereo imaging. There are a number of stereo-microphone techniques that can be used in this respect where the overall goal is to achieve good localisation, so that a sound from centre stage comes from the centre of your stereo speakers. Similarly, a sound from the left would be heard mainly in the left speaker and a sound just to the left of centre would appear to come from just left of the mid-point between your speakers, and so on.

To understand fully how stereo miking may or may not produce realistic sound images we need to understand a bit about how our hearing system works. More information on this can be found in **Acoustics and Psychoacoustics** by D. M. Howard and J. A. S. Angus. *Focal Press*, ISBN: 0-240-51609-5.

The easiest method with which to get good results, while still allowing some experimentation, is the **coincident pair**. For this you need to take two cardioid condenser microphones and position them with their capsules one above another just touching, angled about 120° apart. Cardioid microphones will also help reduce the amount of reverb in your recording, due to the null pickup point at their rear, improving the overall clarity. In general you want a good level of direct sound compared with the reverberant sound. Placing the

If you have two figure-of-eight microphones you can experiment with an excellent stereo miking technique called Blumlein Stereo. This is a variation on the coincident pair in which the two microphones are angled 90° apart pointing to the left and right of your sound source.

Note that you are allowed to use one or two additional mics to capture ambience and reverberation. A type of microphone known as PZM (pressure zone microphone) that has a flat plate designed to be mounted on a wall can be good for this. Whatever you use, balance such sources with your more direct coincident pair to give more control over the finished result. However this does add to the complexity and it is usually best to experiment with your main pair until you get a sound that you like.

mics where you would normally sit in the audience will give too much reverb when listening over loudspeakers. The closer the mics are to your performers, the closer they will sound in the recording. Experiment with distance to achieve the best balance between closeness and clarity, and liveness and reverberance.

Once you have arrived at an optimum distance for your microphones you need to consider the stereo imaging produced by the coincident pair. Monitor the performers over headphones and listen to make sure that what you hear agrees with what you see and hear in the actual venue. If the stereo spread is too wide or too narrow you can adjust the angle of separation. If the image is too off-centre make sure your levels are equal for both mics and that they are pointing in the appropriate direction. If you have a chance, before the performers enter the venue, record yourself talking as you walk across the front of the performance area and listen back to make sure the recorded stereo imaging is in agreement.

Microphones – some general tips

✦ Always use stands that give good stability and allow you to raise the microphones to a good high level. Raising or lowering the mics can also help you achieve balance between soloists and the accompanying ensemble if this is required.

✦ Use shock mounts to prevent noise from vibration. If they are not available place the stands on some rubber or sponge mats (carpet tiles can also be useful).

✦ A good starting position in terms of mic distance and height is about 4m from the musicians and about 4m above the floor.

✦ Keep your mic cables tidy and away from places where they might be stepped on or tripped over. Give yourself some slack at the bottom of the mic stand to allow for repositioning or for someone tripping over a cable.

✦ Check that all filters or level controls on the microphones themselves are set as you wish (or left in bypass mode) and make sure both mics are set the same. Unless you are recording outside (not recommended!) do not use foam shields on microphones as they can attenuate important high frequency detail.

✦ If your mics need batteries always make sure you replace them before a session.

Mixing desk

Once you have selected and positioned the microphones you will need to connect them to the **mixing desk** so that they can be routed to your stereo recorder (although it may be possible to connect the microphones directly without having to use a desk). A mixing desk, whether it is a separate unit or combined with a multitrack recorder, is designed to route and mix audio signals from your microphones and electronic instruments. These signals travel to and from your recorders (both multitrack and two-track mastering), effects units and studio monitoring devices (speakers or headphones, both for you – the engineer/producer – and for the performers).

When recording, the mixer is used to set and control recording levels and send your audio signals to the individual tracks of your multi-track recorder. When mixing down, the audio tracks have their levels set relative to each other; they are combined, altered using effects where necessary and sent to the stereo master recorder.

All mixing desks follow a similar design, and usually consist of one set of physical components repeated over and over again (the mixer channels). It is well worth spending time studying the manual that comes with your particular mixing desk to understand the particular set of features it offers. However the following paragraphs outline some of the features common to all desks.

Computer-based software mixers are similar to their hardware equivalents. You will find them in most computer-based recording and sequencing packages.

Input section – the channel strip

The input channels allow you to adjust the properties of a single input signal, from a microphone or an electronic source. The channels are usually vertical strips of controls lined up side by side and are always the same. Once you understand one you therefore understand most of your mixer. The more channels you have, the more instruments or microphones you can connect and record at the same time. A channel will typically have the following sections:

There are usually at least three input sockets per channel: a three-pin XLR cable MIC input (which can also be used for **DI** boxes) and two ¼-inch jack inputs, one being the LINE input for synthesisers etc, the other being the TAPE input for signals from the multitrack recorder. You may also find an additional stereo jack input called the INSERT (or a pair of jack sockets labelled SEND and RETURN) to allow you to connect compressors and similar effects units. Input selection buttons allow you to choose which physical input you wish to work with, MIC, LINE or TAPE.

Once your signal has entered the desk a preamp will boost the relatively weak microphone signal to a level suitable for processing through the mixing desk. The amount of boost is controlled by the gain (or trim) control, which allows you to adjust the signal level for the best compromise between noise (too low) and distortion (too high). It is used to adjust the recording level of your signal.

The equalisation (EQ) controls allow you to adjust the tonal quality of your signal across bass, treble and midrange frequency bands.

The Auxiliary (or Effect sends) section allows you to create a submix which can be sent (via a master auxiliary output) to an effects unit or to the performers' headphones to provide them with foldback.

The pan pot is used to vary the left-right position of your input signal in the stereo field and is also used in routing (see below).

Routing switches allow you to select where your input signal goes within the desk. Usually this will be to the main stereo MIX bus so that you can actually hear your input sound. However you may also wish to send the signal to a particular group or recorder track. Usually the routing switches will send a signal to a *pair* of groups/tracks (eg tracks 1 and 2). You then use the pan control to set whether the signal goes to 1 only (pan hard left), 2 only (pan hard right) or both equally (pan to the centre).

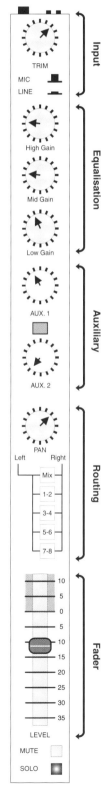

The fader is the largest control on the input channel and is used to adjust the level of the signal. When recording, set the fader to its zero-level mark and adjust the recording level using the gain control. When mixing down, the gain control is bypassed and the fader is used to balance the relative levels of your tracks.

Output section

This part of the mixing desk signal path allows you to determine the destinations of all your input signals. It will include:

Master faders Usually a pair of faders controlling the overall level of the stereo mix leaving the desk for your stereo master-recorder. Normally these will be set to their optimum zero-level mark and then can be left alone, apart from fading the whole track in or out.

Groups Larger desks have an additional set of faders often called groups or subgroups. They can be used to group together lots of similar sounds under one control when mixing (eg eight channels of drumkit to a single fader). If you are using a separate multitrack recorder the groups are usually connected to the inputs of each track. An input signal is sent to a group using the routing switches present on each channel.

Master effects sends and returns In the same way that each channel fader must run through the master fader before it leaves the desk, each aux or effects-send signal from a channel must run through a similar master level control that will be found in the output section of the desk. You may also have a set of dedicated effects returns that allow your effected signal to be mixed in with the dry signal before it is output to your stereo master-recorder.

Level meters These measure the level of the signals going through each output bus and are an important guide to helping you set recording and mixing levels. Usually they take the form of a column of multi-coloured LEDs and you should ensure your levels are in the 0 to +6dB range (with a digital desk you should never reach the maximum possible level of 0dB).

Monitor section

This section allows you to control what you and your performers listen to and it is completely independent of the signal going to your master recorder. When recording you want to monitor your input signals. During playback or mixing down you will want to monitor the multitrack inputs, and when overdubbing a combination of both. Your mixer may have a number of controls called Mon Mix, Tape Cue or similar and they may be completely separate from the input channels (a *split* mixing desk design) or they might form a small part of each input channel (an *inline* mixing desk). These controls will usually consist of just a basic level control, but may also include pan, **EQ** and one or two aux sends. You may also find dedicated buttons or controls allowing you to set up mixes for the main control-room speakers, headphones or for your performers. These allow you to monitor the output from your stereo mastering machine without having to do any repatching. Again, see your mixing-desk manual for the exact features available to you.

Recording

Once you have set up your microphones and connected them to your two-track, either directly or via a mixing desk, you are almost ready to start recording. Try to listen to your performers using high quality, studio nearfield speakers in a separate room. If this is not possible use the best-quality headphones you can find, preferably of the type that have a closed back and surround the ear, preventing spill from your headphones leaking into the microphones and also giving you some isolation from the performers themselves.

It is critical to get a good signal level when recording. When using a digital medium your level meters should be registering around the -15dB to -12dB region most of the time, with peaks reaching up as far as -3dB. This will still give you some headroom should there be any particularly loud passages, but you should never reach 0dB as this will produce harsh digital distortion. Ask the performers to run through the piece before the actual take so that you can check levels and adjust them accordingly. You shouldn't have to change them during the actual recording itself. If your recorder has a peak hold function, it will help you keep a close eye on what is happening with the signal levels. Sometimes a performer will often play louder when they know they are actually being recorded so you should listen out for this and adjust levels accordingly to compensate.

Since you will already have taken time to position and balance your microphones, the left and right meters on your recorder or desk should be registering about the same levels. If you are routing your microphones via a mixing desk make sure that the channels are panned appropriately and have the same gain levels set at the input stage to give a balanced stereo field.

Remember to keep detailed notes (and diagrams where applicable) as to what happens during your session for your recording log. This should include the timings of your recordings and where they occur on your mastering medium, microphone choice and placement considerations, performer placement, equipment lists, settings and connections, venue details, together with any problems you encountered and how you dealt with them. This will be especially useful if you cannot complete everything in one session and you have to repeat some of your preparatory work. Always label your tapes, CDs, etc and make backup copies as soon as possible in case of data corruption, loss or damage of the original.

Remember to make full use of the studio time available. You should aim for several good takes in case blemishes on one are not noticed until later. The performers will need several complete run-throughs before they reach their best, and these may also give you the opportunity to experiment with different mic positions and balance settings.

Evaluation

Once you have completed your recording take it to your studio control room or other similar listening space so that you can audition the finished results. Listen carefully to your work, asking yourself the questions printed in the list on the next page. Based on this assessment you may wish, time and circumstances permitting, to go back and do another recording session. If not, prepare your finished recording for submission, making sure that you use the full dynamic range of the medium via **normalisation** when you are working in the digital domain. You may also need to top and tail the recording to remove any extraneous noise immediately before or after the piece.

Evaluation checklist

+ Can I hear any background noise?
+ Can I hear any distortion?
+ Are the left and right channels balanced equally?
+ Have I made good use of the dynamic range of the recording medium? (Are the recording levels too high or too low?)
+ Have I accurately captured the stereo field of the sound sources?
+ Is the recording too reverberant or too dry?
+ Do the microphones capture the sound sources well in terms of frequency range, and imaging and positioning?
+ Can I hear each instrument clearly?
+ Is the recording a good representation of the performance?
+ Do I enjoy listening to my recording?

Multitrack recording

Planning a session

When recording direct to two-track, your task as engineer and producer is to capture the performance of your ensemble almost as if the listeners were present in the venue themselves. When working with a multitrack in the popular/jazz style a rather different approach is required. The medium you are now working in becomes an integral part of the creative process allowing you to experiment with arrangements, ideas and creative effects. You can also rerecord individual instrumental tracks in isolation, a bar at a time if need be, until they are perfect. With all of this control, the key to a successful session, and ultimately to satisfactorily completing your work for this assessment, is planning and preparation.

Venue

Because close-mic techniques are used when recording popular music, the acoustic qualities of your venue are not as critical as they were with your classical direct to stereo recording. However you will still need to consider issues relating to noise, both leaking into your recordings from outside and from your performers instruments (often amplified) annoying those in close proximity. You will also need to think about how you are going to arrange yourself and your equipment (if you do not have a dedicated studio). You should be able to monitor your performers accurately during recording without having to worry about sound levels making this difficult or having your movements or comments being picked up over the microphones.

Choice of piece

As with the two-track work your choice of piece will depend on what your available musicians can reliably perform. You may also have to consider what instruments or additional equipment will be required (amps, drum kits etc). Keep your work relatively simple wherever possible, with a basic four-piece jazz or pop ensemble consisting of guitar, bass, drums and vocals being ideal.

Direct injection

A DI box allows you to connect an instrument directly to your mixing desk or recorder without having to use a microphone. This can speed up the recording process, allowing more than one track to be laid down at a time without having to worry about spill, and avoids the difficulties associated with selecting and placing microphones. Electronic instruments such as keyboards can be connected directly to the line input of your mixing desk. Bass guitars are often recorded using DI – either from a Direct Out connection from the guitarist's amp, or via a DI box, which allows the guitar to be plugged directly into the desk without any amp at all. Compare direct and miked-up versions wherever possible to see which sounds the best for your recording. You shouldn't really DI the electric guitar as the speaker in the guitar amp is a fundamental part of the overall sound. However DI can be good for very clear, clean guitar sounds, or extreme and unnatural distorted sounds.

The recent influx of guitar 'amp modelling' products provides an alternative solution to DI recording with excellent natural results. For examples of this technology see: http://www.line6.com/

When you have more information about the piece of music that you will be recording, the performers involved and instruments used, you should start to plan how you will distribute microphones and instruments across your mixer channels.

Mixer channels

Even more important than assigning instruments to mixer channels is assigning instruments to tracks on your recorder. It may well be the case that you have more performers or instruments than you do tracks. If so you will have to decide carefully at this early stage how you will organise them. This will also influence the order of recording and indicate whether you may need to make use of **bouncing** in order to have enough tracks available (see page 60).

Recorder tracks

Discuss with your performers how they wish to record their piece. They may wish to tackle it one instrument at a time or prefer to record the whole band at once and then overdub individual tracks. With the former method the drums are often recorded first as the rhythm will form the foundation of the whole piece. If this is the case you may have to prepare a guide on a spare track. This could be a click generated from a metronome or sequencer, or one of the other members of the ensemble doing a rough version of their part that can be recorded over later to give the drummer (and subsequent performers) something to play against.

Order of recording

A track sheet is used to keep a record of mixer channels, tape tracks, times and the parts recorded. It will prove helpful in organising your sessions and when writing-up your recording log. A good example for free download is available from: http://www.soundcraft.com/learning/learning.html

If the whole band insists on playing together, select which instruments you wish to record first (again often drums and maybe a directly-injected bass) and decide how you are going to arrange your performers to avoid spill. You may be able to have the rest of the band in the control room if there is space. Those performances that are not critical at this stage can be mixed down to one track and will serve as a suitable guide track for overdubbing purposes.

You will need to provide adequate **foldback** for your performers so they can hear a mix of both themselves and what you have recorded so far (either guide tracks or performance tracks), so that they can play along. This will usually be provided by a suitable output from your mixer and should be presented over headphones, preferably with a closed back to prevent spill into the recording mics. If you are recording a number of performers at the same time they will each require a mix, and you will also need some means of communicating with them. On purpose-built studio desks this is often provided by a talkback microphone built into the desk. If you do not have this facility a microphone plugged into a spare channel routed through to their headphones will work fine.

Foldback

As with your classical assignment, ensuring you make good use of your recording levels at all stages of the process is critical. You may need a compressor with some instruments to get a more consistent overall recording level (see the section later on Effects).

Recording levels

Backup

Finally, when organising your sessions and looking after your recording medium, plan your backup procedures. Allow time at the end of a session to backup your work so that it always exists in at least two physically different places at any one time. This should be true from your very first session to the completion of your final two-track mixdown. A good idea is to have two tapes or discs. Use one as your work in progress and the other as your backup medium that you copy to at the end of every session.

Microphone selection and positioning

Close-miking is commonly used in pop and jazz recordings. It helps create impact, reduces spill between instruments (if more than one is being recorded at the same time) and means you don't have to worry so much about the quality of the acoustics of the room in which you are recording. The correct selection and positioning of your microphone is, however, still a critical factor in the overall quality of the recorded results. In this section we will look briefly at some of the most common instruments you will most likely have to record – vocals, guitar (acoustic and electric) and drums.

Vocals

The lead vocal in popular music is usually the focal point of the piece, carrying the melody and possibly a narrative, and often a great part of the compositional intent. As such it is critical to record it well. In general the microphone to use is the best one you have available, usually a cardioid condenser preferably with a large diaphragm. The cardioid pattern will give a close sound with good rejection of room reverberation. You might want to try an omni-directional pattern for a more open and natural sound if the room is not very reverberant. Dynamic microphones sometimes work well on more powerful male vocal tracks.

If your vocalist is used to performing live they may try to sing very close to the microphone to use proximity effect to make their voice sound full and more powerful. This is not desirable in a studio situation and it is important to ensure your vocalist maintains their distance from the microphone. A good general position for the microphone is a hand-span away from the head at eye level, which will also help to minimise breath noise and 'popping'.

Popping is caused when words containing the letter 'p' (and to a lesser extent 't') cause a small blast of air to hit the microphone resulting in distortion and level peaking. The best way to minimise this undesirable effect is to use a **pop shield**, which you can make yourself from an old wire coat hanger with a nylon stocking stretched over it – this is always preferable to the foam shield supplied with microphones. If you attach this shield to a spare mic stand you can use it as a barrier to distance your vocalist from the microphone and stop them getting any closer than is required.

Other problems to look out for include exaggerated sibilance (over-emphasis of 's' and 'sh' sounds) and reflections from flat surfaces. Sibilance can be reduced by using a mic with a flat frequency response in the 5kHz–10kHz region, and sometimes in this case a dynamic may be preferable to a condenser. Reflections may be picked up by the microphone from a music stand or a nearby wall, leading to interference with the direct sound, and your positioning should take these factors into account.

Guitars

The characteristic sound of the electric guitar consists of several elements – the guitar itself, any effects pedals used (such as wah-wah or distortion), the amplifier and loudspeaker. The traditional way to capture this sound is by miking up the loudspeaker at the end of this signal chain (see also the notes on DI, on page 50). Usually a cardioid dynamic microphone is selected, typically with a presence peak (a boost around 5kHz) in its frequency response to add 'bite'. This offers a focused sound with minimum spill and will handle a high dynamic level without distortion. As a starting point, place the microphone about an inch away from the speaker grille, just off to one side of the centre of the actual cone. You can experiment with different types of microphone and with positioning to get a sound you like.

A similar approach can be taken for recording the bass guitar if you decide not to DI (although for a clean and well-defined sound this may be the best option). Any condenser or dynamic mic with a good low frequency response should suffice and you can use a similar positioning strategy. Whereas effects are a fundamental part of a guitar player's sound, it is often best to record the bass with no effects at all (apart from perhaps some compression), as reverb or delay can often confuse and muddy the sound.

A condenser microphone should be your first choice for the acoustic guitar – either cardioid or omnidirectional according to the reverberation characteristics of the room and the type of sound you are after. The guitar body projects different tones at different points, so careful microphone positioning is critical for an accurate recorded representation. The best place to start is about 15–30cm away from where the fingerboard joins the body. If you are recording an electro-acoustic guitar always use a microphone rather than the guitar output (unless the guitar itself is of very poor quality) as this will give a much more warm, natural and rewarding sound.

Whatever the type of guitar, think carefully about the instrument you are recording and the equipment you are using. Old strings, poorly maintained pickups and electronics, bad leads, excessive amplifier gain, mains hum and old batteries in effects units will all have a detrimental effect on the final result which you won't be able to fix in the mix. Negotiate with your performers to get the best out of them and their instruments. Always check tunings before a take, and if possible turn off any overhead strip lights or computer monitors as these will interfere with the guitar pickups and appear as noise in your finished recording.

Drums

A drum kit is perhaps the most difficult of instruments to record well in the studio, due to the fact that it consists of a number of very different individual instruments, each with its own distinct timbre and characteristics, all working together in close proximity. The starting point is to ensure the kit sounds as good as possible. This includes tuning the individual drums, taping down any hardware that rattles, damping drum heads if they 'ring' too much and taping the underside of cymbals to avoid too much brightness. There are two methods of microphone rigging that can be used to capture the sound of the kit, based on the overall conception of the recording and the sound you require.

Damping drum heads often improves the general tone of the snare drum or tom-tom and can be achieved by taking a small square wad of tissues or folded material and taping three sides of it to one side of the drum skin. Don't damp the head too much or the sound will lose much of its resonant quality and sound dull and lifeless.

The first and most popular method is to close-mike each part of the kit as if it were an individual instrument:

✦ Kick drum. A cardioid dynamic microphone with a good low-frequency response and preferably a large diameter should be placed on a short stand and mounted in the kick drum itself. Always dampen the drum sound by using a weighted-down blanket (or similar). An old credit card taped to the skin in front of the beater helps to reinforce the sharp, hard percussive click of the beat if so required. The egg-shaped AKG D112 is the traditional choice of microphone for kick drums.

✦ Snare drum. A good choice is a cardioid dynamic microphone with a presence peak (such as a Shure SM57/58), using the proximity effect to give a fuller sound and the peak to add attack. Boom the mic in from the front of the kit, about 2cm from the rim and 2–4cm above and angled across the head. Make sure it is out of the way of the drummer's sticks and angled as far away from the hi-hat as possible.

+ Hi-hat. Use a cardioid condenser microphone to pick up the hi-end content and more delicate transient stick work. Place the mic above the hi-hat, pointing down on the edge furthest away from the drummer. Angle the mic slightly away from the kit to further reduce spill. Don't mike from the side since when the hi-hat closes it produces a puff of air that can cause popping.

+ Tom-toms. Cardioid dynamics are a good choice, miking each drum individually, or using one mic per pair. Position about 2cm from the rim and 2cm above, and angle the mic across the drum head out of range from the drummer's sticks.

+ Cymbals. Cymbals are usually picked up on two overhead mics working in stereo about 1m above the outside edges of the cymbals on either side of the kit. A pair of good cardioid condensers with a flat and extended high-frequency response is the best choice, being sure to place them so that they pick up all the cymbals evenly. Another good option, particularly for a mono drum mix is a coincident pair behind and above the drummer's head.

This gives considerable control over each sound source, with the potential for additional individual effects processing. However the luxury of control comes at the expense of complexity. Your ability to mike each part of the kit individually will depend on how many microphones and mixer channels you have available. Further, you would need at least a 16-track recorder to enable you to record each part of the kit individually and still leave room for your other tracks. For eight-track recording you would have to sub-mix the drum kit to stereo, possibly sub-mixing to mono for a four-track recording. This implies that you have to make decisions early in the recording process, possibly without hearing the drum kit within the context of the whole mix. The close proximity of each component of the drum kit also implies that spill will be a problem. As a result cardioid pattern microphones are usually selected, although this can lead to problems of off-axis colourisation (as each microphone will to some extent pick up sounds from other parts of the kit around it) and **phase cancellation**. However, the results can be very rewarding, leading to powerful kick- and snare-drum sounds at the front of the mix, crisp, rhythmic hi-hats and controlled cymbal hits.

Off-axis colourisation is an undesirable side effect to consider when using cardioid type microphones. They have a good frequency response from the front but it becomes more non-linear when a sound moves round to the sides (or off the main axis), leading to unwanted tonal colouration.

The second method of miking a drum kit is much simpler. Good results can be achieved quickly and easily with a coincident pair placed high above the drummer's head, pointing down at the kit. This technique, which is often used in jazz recordings, gives even coverage and a natural stereo image. An additional microphone for the kick drum is also desirable. Again you must make sure that the kit sounds good as a whole prior to miking it up, as there will be little opportunity to correct mistakes with additional processing and EQ as you can when close-miking. Close-miking a drum kit is an excellent recording exercise, and it allows the use of some dramatic effects, but if it is done quickly and without much thought then considerable time may have to be spent during mixdown to get each part to sound right in the overall mix. If only limited time is available to complete your work always opt for the overheads plus additional supporting kick-drum mic option.

Effects

Effects can be used to correct or enhance your recordings and are generally used at the mixdown stage. You can use them as you record, and indeed with instruments such as the electric guitar they are an essential part of the recorded sound, but you have to be quite sure about the sound you are after because once an instrument has been recorded with a particular effect you can't change or remove the effect without re-recording the original. Effects can be used to correct or enhance elements of a recording, or they can be employed as a creative tool to produce new or varied timbres based on your original source sounds.

There are many different effects available, but in this section we will look briefly at three of the most important: EQ, compression and reverb. Again, experimentation is the key to becoming expert in their use, and although it is often tempting to get carried away with the use of original and exciting effects, less is very often more, and no amount of additional effects can hide a poor performance or a badly made recording.

Equalisation, or EQ as it is more commonly known, allows you to adjust the relative balance of the frequencies present in your audio recording. EQ controls are usually found on each channel of even the most basic mixing desks. More expensive desks give you more EQ sections or 'bands' per channel, but the least you should expect are low, high and mid. Low and high (more commonly known as bass and treble) are designed to allow you to cut or boost all the frequencies above or below a specific point. Typically a low EQ will be set to cut or boost frequencies below 100Hz, and a high EQ will do a similar task above 10kHz. The mid-range between these two extremes is then controlled using one (or more) bands of mid EQ. These controls alter a specific range of frequencies around a central value. This central value may be fixed (usually at around 1000Hz), but most desks allow you to vary it, dialling in any value you wish within the mid-range you are listening to. These types of EQ are generally called sweepable mids. They have two controls – a gain control (which works over a frequency range set around a central point), and a frequency control which allows you to select the centre frequency around which the cut or boost will occur.

Three good guidelines for using EQ are:

1. Cut rather than boost. Your ears are more likely to notice a sound being turned up rather than being turned down. Also remember that boosting runs the risk of adding distortion. For example if you want to make your track more bass heavy, don't boost the low gain, try cutting the high gain instead – it will give a more subtle way of obtaining essentially the same result.

2. If you think of mixing your tracks together as painting a picture with sound then the high and low EQ controls are the broad brushstrokes, capable of bold but often brash and unrefined statements. The fine detail is done with your sweepable mid EQ and you should use this in preference wherever possible, as you will then have far more detailed control over your audio soundscape and will obtain a much better finished result.

EQ

The diagram below shows the frequency response of high and low EQ together with a single sweepable mid control:

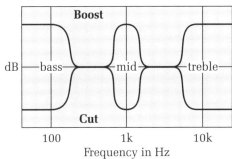

A good way to get used to what the various bands of EQ do, how they interact and what they sound like, is to play a CD you know well through your mixer. Listen to how the sound changes as a result of adjusting EQ. Once you have made some recordings of your own, experiment in the same way with individual instrument sounds. Using your EQ controls you should be able to work out the effective frequency ranges of the various instruments you have recorded.

3. Always listen to your EQ settings within the context of the whole mix. What sounds good in isolation may not work with everything else around it.

Compression

Compression is a very subtle and often misunderstood effect that is fundamental to the production of popular music. Unlike classical music, most pop music has a very limited dynamic range – there is little difference in level between loud and quiet passages.

Essentially a **compressor** is an automatic volume control, turning down the signal level when it gets too loud. As a result of the loudest parts of your recording being compressed, you can afford to turn up the overall signal level knowing that it won't distort or clip. Therefore a compressor can be said to make the louder parts of your recordings quieter and the quiet parts louder, hence reducing the overall dynamic range.

Listen to some pop CDs through your mixer, making sure the left and right channels are balanced, and observe the level meters – they should remain quite consistent around 0dB, even where just one or two instruments are playing. Why doesn't the singer get drowned out or the meter levels shoot up when the rest of the band enters? (Imagine the increase in volume if they were playing live!). In a live concert why does the level of the singer's voice remain constant even if they are not good at holding the microphone directly in front of their mouth? The answer is down to the use of compression, resulting in the reduction of the dynamic range of the source and a more consistent overall signal level.

Compressors are in-line effects, applied to single sound sources on single mixing desk channels only (or across two stereo channels if the compressor has a stereo mode) via the individual channel insert points. They are very useful when recording acoustic sources, particularly vocals, as a small amount of compression will enable you to get a consistently high recording level without having to worry about clipping or manually adjusting the gain controls during a take. Compression on bass guitar gives an even and consistent feel to the sound, and it can be used on a drum kit to give sounds more impact and even-out the levels between, for instance, snare hits if the drummer has a somewhat inconsistent style.

As with EQ, it is worth understanding how the controls of a compressor work, especially as the processed sound from a compressor is more subtle and less dramatic than that from an EQ section. The main functions are:

✦ Threshold. Your audio signal is compressed according to a level that you set using the threshold control: below this level the compressor does nothing, but as soon as the signal goes over the threshold then the compressor will start to reduce the gain of the signal. A setting of -10dB is a good value to start with for very subtle compression, -20dB will be a bit more noticeable.

✦ Ratio. This refers to how the output level changes in relation to the input level. 2:1 means that for every 2dB change in the input level there will be a 1dB change in the output level. ∞:1 means the output level will never go above the threshold level. A ratio of 3:1 is a good starting point.

✦ The gain-reduction meter shows by how many dB the input is being reduced. A higher ratio or lower threshold means more gain reduction. For basic level control or subtle compression you should see nothing more than 6dB of gain reduction.

✦ Attack time. This refers to how fast the compressor reduces the gain after the signal has passed the threshold level. A fast attack will compress all the peaks, giving an even signal level. A longer attack time will allow fast transient sounds to pass through uncompressed, giving a percussive and punchy sound with impact.

◆ The release time refers to how long it takes for the compressor to return to normal after a loud signal has passed. Short release times keep a good control of the signal and give a good high average level but can result in an audible 'pumping' of the sound as the compressor is being constantly activated and reset. Long release times can result in the compressor always being active, even during quieter passages.

◆ Output level. So far the compressor has only served to reduce the louder peaks in your audio signal. The output-level control now allows you to boost the level of the signal leaving the compressor before it returns to your mixer channel, thus compensating for the overall gain reduction you have applied. This effectively makes the quieter sections of your recordings louder, increasing the overall average signal level and giving a more consistent and professional result. Start with the output level at 0dB and then adjust it to suit the amount of gain reduction you are applying.

Three useful tips for using compression are:

1. If you decide to use a compressor during recording it is usual to set it to be quite transparent, so that it only works on excessive level peaks. Again this is because you can't remove compression once it has been recorded, but you can always add more if required at the mixdown stage.

2. Most compressors have two sets of LED meters indicating output level and gain reduction. These are a great help in showing you the amount of compression being applied and how the attack and release controls are set.

3. Most compressors have an auto button that sets the attack and release controls for you – they follow the dynamics of the music so that they are always at the best average setting. If you are not sure about using attack and release settings leave auto on when recording until you are more confident in their use.

Reverb

The process of close-miking in popular music recording means that there is usually little of the recording room's acoustic characteristics in the finished result and so artificial reverb has to be added at the mixing-down stage. Reverb can sound dramatic and exciting, and it can help notes and passages blend together into a uniform event. However too much can make your music lack clarity and sound cluttered. Reverb can also impart a sense of distance. If you turn up your aux send to increase the proportion of reverberant sound to direct sound, it will have the effect of moving your sound source further away in your artificial reverberant hall. It will become less clear and appear to be in the background of your mix.

A reverb or multi-effects unit is connected to your mixer in a different way from a compressor. Each channel of the mixer should have at least one auxiliary (or effects send) control. Find the output socket for this on the back of your mixer and connect it to the input of the reverb unit. Connect the outputs from the reverb unit to the aux or effects returns on the mixer. Note that if you do not have specific effects returns, a couple of spare channels panned left and right will serve just as well. Set the mix control on the reverb unit to 100% wet or 100% reverb, as you will control the balance of reverberated (wet) and unreverberated (dry) signals using the mixing desk itself. Turn the master aux control about three-quarters up, and set the aux return controls to about 0dB. You can now adjust the amount of reverb on each track by turning up the appropriate individual aux send control.

Most reverb settings are self-explanatory (eg big hall, small hall and room) but some are worthy of further explanation:

+ Plate reverb. Before digital reverberation became commonplace, artificial reverb was generated by passing the dry audio signal through a large metal plate. This produced a very bright sound that most modern reverb units can replicate.

+ Reverse reverb. A reverberant sound that fades in and builds up rather than the usual fade out and decay.

+ Gated reverb. The reverb is cut off quickly before it has a chance to decay. Very dramatic when used on drums and characteristic of many of the drum tracks on songs recorded in the 1980s.

+ Early reflections. An effect where an ambience is produced by modelling the first few sound reflections from the walls of a room, rather than the dense decaying reverberant tail. More subtle than reverb, giving a natural sense of space without cluttering up your mix.

Reverberation consists of complex reflections which, as they fade away, have the effect of prolonging the original sound. This is not the same as an echo, which is a distinct repetition of a sound. Echo (or delay) is an effect that can add life and syncopation to a track, although like reverb, if used too much can clutter your overall mix. For best results set the delay time relative to the tempo of your piece (some units allow you to set the delay time automatically by tapping along with the tempo using a control on the front panel). Very short delay times (15–35ms) can be used for automatic double tracking (**ADT**) effects to make an instrument or voice sound fuller. But better still is to **double-track** your lead instrument or vocal by recording it again onto a spare track.

A useful tip is to use reverberation to help your vocalists. Set up their headphone mix with a little reverb on the voice – it will help them to sing better and more in tune. However don't include this effect on the actual recording – reverberation should be added later during mixdown.

Preparing for mixdown

You will need to decide which of your successful takes to use for your master. Try to involve the performers in the decision – when they listen in detail they may even feel that a further take would be worthwhile before the session ends.

It is best not to attempt a mixdown as soon as the session has finished. Rough and final mixes should be done when your ears are fresh. Before starting it is a good idea to listen to some of your favourite commercial CDs through the studio monitoring system, as you will get some idea of how the monitoring system alters a sound played through it in terms of bass, middle and treble. Think also about the production used on the CD, in terms of the balance of the instruments and how effects have been used.

Mixing down

Mixing down is the task of bringing together your recorded tracks into one finished, coherent musical work on an appropriate two-track master. A good starting point is to pan everything to the centre, bring all your faders up to the 0dB mark, and then adjust to suit, making the most important tracks louder and the background tracks quieter. Alternatively, bring each track in one at a time and balance up the current track relative to the previous one. The best instruments to start with are those that form the foundation for your piece – usually drums, then bass, then guitars or keyboards and finally lead instruments and/or vocal. Try to aim for clarity – you should be able to hear each instrument clearly, but without one dominating the mix. The vocal in particular should be clear and well presented.

The method described here is just one way of working. You may instead decide to produce a preliminary mix of just the backing tracks over which, once complete, you then overdub a vocal or instrumental soloist.

Mixing tips

✦ Zero the mixing desk before you start. EQ should be flat, aux sends turned down and channels should be routed to stereo/mix. Bring down the faders on any channels not in use.

✦ Set levels as high as possible for the multitrack returns, effects sends and returns, external effects units and (most importantly) for your two-track mastering machine.

✦ Group logical sections of your mix, such as the drum kit, so that you can control the overall level of the grouped elements from a single fader or pair of faders.

✦ Go through each track/channel one at a time and apply corrective effects such as compression or EQ. Remember to listen to the track in isolation and as part of the whole mix as you do this.

✦ Don't overdo the effects, especially reverb, as this can clutter your recording and take away the contrast that is needed to give your mix punch.

✦ Create a good sense of stereo width by panning your tracks. Careful use of panning will allow your tracks to sit together better in the mix, rather than all fighting for the same sonic area and ending up sounding confused. Don't pan bass sounds such as kick drums or bass guitars.

✦ Try panning your sounds from left to right as you might imagine them on a stage playing live.

✦ Try not to have too many instruments competing for the same part of the frequency spectrum. You can improve separation when mixing by using EQ.

✦ Don't over-equalise tracks as they're likely to sound unnatural, especially when boosted.

✦ Compress the vocals to make them sit nicely in the mix.

✦ Don't monitor too loudly.

✦ Check your mixes on headphones as well as speakers. Headphones show up some details that you might not hear over loudspeakers. Don't rely solely on headphones for mixing, as they represent the stereo image differently to loudspeakers and have a poor low-frequency response.

+ In a busy mix, try 'ducking' mid-range instruments such as guitars and synths, so that whenever vocals are present the conflicting sounds fall in level slightly. This will work better than just turning up the vocals to make them louder.

Bouncing down

If you are using a four-track machine for AS (the minimum for A2 is eight-track) you may have to use a technique known as bouncing down, where you mix several recorded tracks to one or two empty tracks, allowing the reclaimed tracks to be used for overdubbing new material. You must be happy with your bounced sub-mix before you record over the original tracks as you won't be able to recover them. You will also have to include any track-specific effects or EQ as part of your bounce. It is best to use bouncing for combining similar timbres, such as backing vocals or separate drum tracks. Don't bounce lead vocals or solo instruments as these should be recorded last on their own tracks, so that you can set levels and use effects to bring the best out of the performance.

Always decide when you intend to do your bounces when you plan your whole session, rather than deciding as you go along. Bouncing enabled early recording engineers and producers such as George Martin and Brian Wilson to commit complex arrangements to tape using only a very limited number of tracks, but these days the technique is rarely used, especially since virtual tracks on hard disk recorders and the bounce-forward operations on some mini-disc machines make it unnecessary.

Evaluation

As with your classical recording you need to evaluate and assess your work. It often helps to listen to your finished mix again a few days after you've completed it, and it is also useful to try it out on as many different sound systems as you can. Compare your mix in the studio with a CD you know well and like. How do they differ? Listen carefully to your work and use the checklist on page 50 to ensure that you haven't missed anything important. For the multi-track project you should also consider:

+ Are the levels consistent throughout the recording?
+ Have I made good use of the stereo field and have I used panning adequately to ensure that it is balanced?
+ Does reverb add a sense of coherence to the piece as a whole, or does it dominate too much and make things seem unclear?
+ Are any of the EQ settings I have used too noticeable?

Save all your mix information and track sheets, including effects settings (all of which can contribute towards your recording log) since you never know what you might want to improve before committing yourself to a final version. After your own assessment you may feel the need to go back and run another recording session or maybe just produce a different remix. If not, prepare your finished recording for submission, being sure to make full use of the dynamic range of the medium via normalisation when you are working in the digital domain. As before remember that you may need to top and tail the recording to remove any extraneous noise immediately before or after the piece, such as spoken count-ins from the band or noises of equipment being switched on or off.

Multitrack recording summary

Recording

1. Turn up headphone/monitor level
2. Monitor the stereo/mix bus
3. Set up a monitor mix for the performers
4. Connect instruments to input channels
5. Select the channel inputs as appropriate
6. Assign channels to tracks
7. Bring up channel, group and master faders
8. Adjust the input gain and set recording levels
9. Record.

Overdubbing

1. Assign instruments/channels to spare tracks
2. Set up monitor mixes for you and your performer(s)
3. Bring up channel, group and master faders
4. Play multitrack
5. Set-up mix of pre-recorded tracks
6. Adjust input gain and set recording levels as performers play along to track
7. Adjust monitor mix to include sound of new instrument being recorded
8. Record new part on spare track
9. Punch in/out as required
10. Bounce tracks if necessary.

Mixing down

1. Set channel inputs to TAPE
2. Monitor the stereo/mix bus
3. Route tape inputs to stereo/mix bus
4. Bring up the master faders
5. Set the pan controls
6. Mix and balance track levels
7. Set EQ and effects
8. Refine mix as appropriate
9. Set master recording levels
10. Record to two-track stereo master.

Finally, remember to back-up your work!

? Private study

1. Explain the difference between a dynamic microphone and a condenser microphone. Which would you choose for recording classical music?

2. What is a coincident pair? What type of microphones would you use for a coincident pair?

3. What is a foldback mix? How would you set one up?

4. What is a pop shield? Why is it important to use one when recording a vocal track in pop music?

5. Explain why a compressor is connected to a mixing desk in a different way to a reverb unit.

6. What is the difference between reverberation and echo?

7. The EQ available on a mixing desk is often complemented by more powerful rack-mounted EQ processors. Can you find out what is meant by each of the following and explain how they might be used? Graphic EQ, Parametric EQ, a high pass (or low cut) filter.

Further reading

Practical Recording Techniques: The Step by Step Approach to Professional Audio Recording by Bruce and Jenny Bartlett. *Focal Press* (second edition). ISBN: 0-240-80306-X.

Good Vibrations, A History of Record Production by Mark Cunningham. *Sanctuary Publishing*. ISBN: 1-86074-242-4.

Recording Techniques for Small Studios by David Mellor. *Sound On Sound (PC Publishing)*. ISBN: 1-870775-29-5.

Recording and Production Techniques for the Recording Musician by Paul White. *Sanctuary Publishing*. ISBN: 1-86074-188-6.

Paul White has also produced a series of short guides, published by *Sound On Sound*. They include *Basic Digital Recording, Basic Mastering, Basic Microphones, Basic Mixers, Basic Mixing Techniques* and *Basic Multitracking*.

Sound On Sound magazine carries many useful articles and reviews. The associated website has an extensive library of online articles from back issues: http://www.sospubs.co.uk/

Harmony Central is another good online resource: http://www.harmony-central.com/

Soundcraft is a British mixing desk manufacturer and produces an excellent guide to mixing and recording. It is available for free download at: http://www.soundcraft.com/learning/learning.html

Arranging and Improvising (AS)

There are two coursework tasks, which must be sent to the examiner by 15 May. They require quite different approaches; one involves the production of a score using sequencing/notating software while the other involves the production of a performance.

Arrangement 1

Starting with a short melody (which may be in any style or from any period) you must extend this into an arrangement for four parts (or tracks) using a computer sequencer. You must then produce a printed score of the arrangement with a separate set of instrumental parts. You must also produce a recording of the work on CD or mini-disc. The following materials must be sent to the examiner:

+ the full score and parts
+ the recording
+ a copy of the original stimulus material.

Arrangement 2

Starting with a song or a melody from a song (which must be a piece of popular music or jazz) you must create a performance involving no fewer than four parts. This can be undertaken in a number of ways:

+ working with a group of musicians in the studio
+ working alone or with other musicians using a portastudio
+ working alone using a computer sequencer.

The specification imposes certain conditions. If you opted for sequencing in the *Sequencing or Recording* component, then you must carry out this task using recording techniques (and you should therefore be sure to have read the chapter starting on page 42). If you opted for recording in the *Sequencing or Recording* component, then you must use sequencing for this task (and you should therefore be sure to have read the chapter starting on page 35).

You must produce a recording of your finished performance on CD or mini-disc. The following materials must be sent to the examiner:

+ the recording
+ a copy of the original stimulus material (either notated or recorded)
+ a written commentary with details of the resources used and the musical intentions.

Introduction

This title of this component, Arranging and Improvising, is a little misleading because improvising, although it plays a part in the preparation of the material for assessment, is not itself assessed as a separate skill. It is best thought of as a production project.

The record producer is more than an engineer. The work of George Martin (who produced the Beatles) and Quincy Jones (who produced Frank Sinatra and Michael Jackson) offers good examples.

Both are highly trained and multi-skilled musicians who can play rock, jazz and classical music, compose, score for orchestra, program the keyboards and drum machines, mike-up the band, run the mixing desk and mix down the final version. The producer's job, then, is to manage the whole process from an initial melody right through to the CD.

Producers work in different ways and this unit reflects this. Some songwriters bring only the most simple of ideas to the studio; a short melody, a couple of lines of lyric and a few guitar chords all of which have to be fleshed out. On the other hand, many rock bands prefer to improvise together in the studio until a good idea comes along and then develop this into a song.

An arrangement usually involves an interpretation of someone else's music. Many musicians in the industry call these versions 'covers' and the two terms, arrangements and covers, are really interchangeable. However a remix involves a slightly different approach, taking a finished product and reworking it in some way, usually quite radically. Remixes are normally associated with club music and it is unlikely that such an approach would be appropriate for this unit unless you chose the materials very carefully and documented the process thoroughly.

Arranging is a subtle art. The goal is to enhance the original rather than provide a transcription in which parts are simply rewritten for different instruments following the original, note for note, chord for chord. For this unit an arrangement needs to go further. Instrumental parts may have to be rewritten idiomatically to suit the change of timbres and there may be other changes too; different harmonies, some new material added, a different stylistic feel.

You should avoid going too far and introducing too many changes. Occasionally students doing an arrangement will extract a fragment of melody or a rhythm and use this as the basis for an entirely new piece. However it is not part of the task to distort or recompose the original, which should always be discernible. The crucial phrase, which you will need to adopt and which is embodied in the mark scheme, is 'faithful to the original'.

Selecting material

The specification lays down exact guidelines to the way you must choose the material for your arrangements.

Arrangement 1

The material you choose can be a folk tune or a melody from a song. It must be longer than 12 bars and it must be available in traditional notation.

You must make the arrangement for at least four instruments, tracks or parts, and you must extend and develop the original into a completed arrangement between 32 and 64 bars long. In addition there must be at least one **modulation** to a contrasting key.

This may seem a rather daunting set of requirements after GCSE but you can adopt tactics which will make the task easier to get started:

- Choose a tune which is simple to notate (eg made up of quavers, crotchets and minims) rather than something syncopated. You can enter these note values relatively easily on the computer using the mouse. Additional material and other parts can be played later in real time.

- Avoid melodies that require many chord changes or complex harmonies – most folk tunes can be harmonised quite simply. A drone is also a common and effective accompaniment but be careful not to over-use this as an excuse for avoiding proper harmony.

- Include the modulation in a middle section. You can devise this section on its own in the new key leaving any linking or bridge passages until later (there are hints on how to do this in the Modulations section on the next page).

- Choose instruments for your arrangement that are easy to notate. Remember that strings and wind are all single-stave instruments whereas keyboards and drums are quite tricky. A full drum kit can be replaced by separate percussion instruments although it is possible to enter a drum-kit part by part (bass drum, snare and hi-hat) and then merge the tracks.

Arrangement 2

The source can be a pop song (or a jazz standard) or a melody from such a song. It must be longer than 16 bars and the original must be commercially available.

You must make the arrangement for at least four instruments, tracks or parts and your completed work must be 32–64 bars long and two to three minutes in duration.

As with Arrangement 1 you can employ some useful tactics:

- Choose a well-known tune for which a recording and sheet music are easily available.

- Be careful not to over-stretch your resources. Stay within the technical limitations of the equipment and within the playing limitations of yourself or your musicians – and that includes choosing a key everyone feels comfortable with.

- Keep a note of what you do so you can include the details in your commentary.

Once you have explored these ideas for the two arrangements you can move on to something more ambitious.

Listening

The most valuable preparation for this unit will come from listening to professional arrangements and cover versions. Try to listen to the original and the arrangement one after the other. Keep a note of the differences, identifying exactly which musical elements have been changed in the arrangement and which are the same – melody, harmony, rhythm, structure, instrumentation, texture and stylistic feel. One very important thing to look out for is the tempo, as this plays a significant role in whether or not the music sounds right.

The margin shows some useful websites and there is a list below of popular or 'classic' covers which you can use as a starting point for your listening.

Recent and popular covers

American Pie (Madonna/Don Mclean)
Always On My Mind (Pet Shop Boys/Elvis Presley)
Killing me Softly With His Song (Fugees/Roberta Flack)
You Can't Hurry Love (Phil Collins/Supremes)

Classic cover CDs

David Bowie *Pin Ups* (covers of sixties rock)
George Martin *In My Life* (covers of the Beatles)
Monty Alexander *Stir it Up* (jazz covers of Bob Marley)

Orchestral and jazz

Tubular Bells (Bedford/Oldfield)
Pictures at an Exhibition (Ravel/Mussorgsky)
Peer Gynt Suite (Duke Ellington/Grieg)
Concerto de Aranjuez (Miles Davis/Rodrigo)

Harmony

One of the most important skills you will need to develop is the ability to harmonise a melody. There are a number of exercises you can do to help:

✦ Practise playing through the chords of songs, either by following a recording or by reading through charts and lead-sheets. Note any special features like key changes.

✦ Try humming a folk tune or a melody that you know well and then, with a guitar or keyboard, try fitting chords to it. Try several versions with alternative chords.

✦ Enter a short melody on the computer and then experiment with chords to fit.

✦ Devise a short chord sequence and write down the component notes of each of the chords.

✦ Now write out the chords in four parts for four instruments.

Modulations

Another skill you will have to master is that of modulation. A modulation occurs when the music moves temporarily into another key. This is often prepared by a cadence in which the new leading note is introduced, although in popular music it is not uncommon to jump into the new key without any preparation. However, avoid the temptation to use the computer's **transpose** function to raise or lower an entire section mechanically – the result will sound very crude and unnatural.

There are several ways to introduce a modulation:

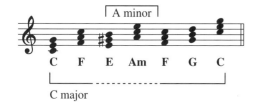

✦ A passing modulation in which the music passes briefly through a key in the middle of a phrase, as in the chord sequence *left*. This is in C major and it passes through A minor (the relative minor of C major). A good way to create a modulation like this is to use the major chord on the fifth note (dominant) of the new key, preferably with a seventh added, followed by the new key chord itself. This is known as a perfect cadence. In our example, the new key is A minor, and its fifth note (dominant) is E.

- A middle section in a contrasting key. Some songwriters jump into the new key and others prepare it with a cadence. The most common keys are the relative minor (or major) and the sub-dominant (the key a 4th higher).

  Another very effective modulation is up a minor 3rd or down a major 3rd. For example if your song is in A major you would jump either into C or F for the middle section. The problem is returning to the home key again because it is not as easy to jump back. You need to devise a short chord progression which ends on the dominant harmony of the home key and thus facilitates the return.

- Some songs feature a key change in the final verse or chorus – usually up a semitone which, although quite a crude device, has the effect of creating a climax.

Instrumentation

You will need to familiarise yourself with the character and capabilities of the instruments you intend to use. This includes the range, any special playing techniques (such as the use of string pizzicato and mutes for string and brass instruments), how to notate the instrument (clef, position in system) and any limitations (allowing breathing spaces for wind players).

Also, bear these points in mind:

- Instrumental writing is always more convincing (and easier on the player) when the composer or arranger writes idiomatically for the instruments. Special care has to be taken when using extremes of range or texture. Long passages of very fast music can be difficult for brass players (or strings playing pizzicato). Avoid giving extended passages of very high or very low notes to wind instruments (unless it is a feature of a solo) as these can be tiring to play. Over-use of percussion (apart from a drum kit which normally plays throughout) can clutter up the texture.

- Choice of key is important, although this is often determined by vocal range if there is a singer. G, D and A are popular with string players but they can be harder for saxophonists (who tend to prefer flat keys). Bass players like F♯ and guitarists generally prefer E.

- If you are working on a MIDI arrangement remember that there is a difference between synth voices and their real orchestral counterparts. Patterns which are easy to finger on a MIDI keyboard may be awkward for wind or string players. Also the keyboard takes no account of the range of other instruments. General MIDI timbres include many non-orchestral sounds and 'pads' but if you must write a bass part for flute you need to make it clear that this is for a synthesised flute, since real flutes cannot normally play below middle C.

- Aim for variety in your textures. The parts do not need to be playing all the time and rests are as important as notes. Using different textures, such as a passage for an unaccompanied solo instrument or a duet section for two parts, will add interest.

A good way of learning about instrumentation is to practise making arrangements for your fellow students to play. Discuss with them how the particular characteristics of their instruments can best be exploited. Try to identify the skills (and weaknesses) of each performer so that you can use their individual strengths in your arrangement. Discuss what sorts of things are easy and what are difficult for each instrument, and try some improvising both separately and together. Books that will help with the job of instrumental writing include:

Orchestral Technique by Gordon Jacob. *Oxford University Press*, 3rd edition 1981. ISBN: 0-19-318204-1.

Orchestration by Walter Piston. *W W Norton*, 1955, reprinted by *Gollancz*, 1978. ISBN: 0-575-02602-2.

Orchestration by Cecil Forsyth. *Macmillan*, 1935, reprinted by *Dover Publications* 1986. ISBN: 0-486-24383-4.

Rock, Jazz and Pop Arranging by Daryl Runswick. *Faber and Faber*, 1992. ISBN: 0-571-51108-2.

Sequencing

The sequencer is a very useful tool for experimenting with musical ideas. The chapter on composing (starting on page 83) identifies a number of such techniques.

Arrangement 1 (and also Arrangement 2 if you are permitted to use the sequencing option) might be approached in a variety of ways. You may find you have a bit more freedom with Arrangement 2 since there will be no need to notate the result.

✦ Make sure your harmonisation of the stimulus melody is secure. Record the melody on to a track and then loop it while you try different chords on the keyboard. Aim for a strong bass line.

✦ If you are intend to create a special stylistic feel (like swing jazz or reggae) record a basic backing track and loop it so you can try out different versions of the melody while it plays.

✦ Make a formal plan of how you will extend the source material into a complete arrangement (remembering that Arrangement 1 needs to modulate).

✦ Make a few copies of the source material and try out different instrumental combinations.

✦ Experiment with different ways of compiling the arrangement working in blocks (a section at a time) or in layers (building up the instrumentation). Alternatively you can record the entire melody and then add the accompanying parts – or try this in reverse by recording the entire backing first then adding the melody.

Notation

Arrangement 1 involves preparing a score and printing out parts. The chapter on composing (see page 83) includes some advice on notation but the following general guidance may be helpful.

Computer-generated scores can produce very neat results, but they can also cause many pitfalls, especially if generated from sequencing software. Sequencers are designed to record note lengths very precisely, just as they are played. If those note lengths are then displayed as a musical score, the result can be a rhythmic nightmare. For example, the simple crotchets and minim of the example *left* might appear like this:

As you can see, the computer's results are unacceptably confusing for the performer. Most sequencer software has facilities, such as score quantisation, to help achieve more acceptable results, but you will still need to check the output carefully for eccentric note-lengths, and unnecessary rests and ties.

Software usually handles pitch better than rhythm, but again you must be on your guard for incorrect accidentals (eg A♯ in F major, when the note should be a B♭). Check carefully for anachronisms such as printing low clarinet notes in the bass clef, and excessive leger lines should be avoided, either by using a different clef if appropriate, or by using an 8va sign. In particular, be sure to check that the software is correctly handling parts for instruments whose music should be written an octave higher than it sounds (eg double bass, guitar and bass guitar) or an octave lower than it sounds (eg descant recorder, piccolo).

You will probably need to edit-in the phrasing and articulation that you require, and you must ensure that the staves are labelled with the instruments you intend, and not just track numbers. Most software should be able to produce correct stem directions and accurate beaming (grouping of notes), but again you should check that you have the right settings for the music concerned.

You will also need to know how your software handles repeats. In all probability it will print the music out again in full, when what is really required is a repeat sign or a *da capo* direction, perhaps with first- and second-time bars in order to differentiate between alternative endings.

Check if any instruments you have used are transposing – such as the clarinet in B♭ or trumpet in B♭, both of which will require their parts printed a tone higher than they sound (they can appear at sounding pitch in the score, but not in the parts). If an instrument rests for more than a few bars, multiple rests should be collapsed into one or more multiple-rests (see *right*). Don't forget that global directions, such as tempo, need to appear in every part.

Most of these problems can be overcome by careful study of the software manual, but remember that it is most unlikely that you will be able merely to press the print button in order to achieve an acceptably accurate score.

If you include a vocal part in Arrangement 2, take special care with the underlay (the positioning of the text under the music). There must be at least one note for every syllable of the text and the words should be aligned *precisely* under the notes to which they apply. Syllables should be divided by hyphens and continuation lines used if several notes are to be sung to a single syllable. One common fault is to try to split single-syllable words with a hyphen, as shown in the example, *right*.

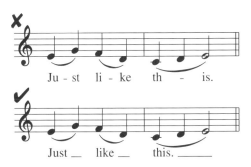

There is clearly a great deal to consider in producing acceptable notation, and you should not leave this task until the last minute. The following points should help you plan your work:

✦ Before you start, identify any gaps in your knowledge of music theory and do something about them. Familiarise yourself with your software; how to format, how to set up drum parts, how to transpose and extract parts.

✦ Keep sight of the fact that you have to produce a score *and* a recording. Use the save-as function to save two versions of the arrangement – one for the score and another for the recording – which you can then work on separately. This is important because any adjustments you make to the sounds might otherwise cause problems with the notation.

+ Alternatively you could consider saving the tracks as a MIDI file and then working with two separate programs – a specialist notation program for the score and a sequencing program for the recording.

+ As with all computing tasks, remember to save, save, save (and then make a back-up disk!).

+ You will probably have entered the arrangement by playing the tracks in real time. If so, you will have to correct any playing errors by quantising the note values, erasing mistakes, correcting wrong notes and deleting doubled noteheads before you are able to edit the details.

+ If you have chosen a swing-feel remember that you can notate the music in straight rhythms and need only to add the written direction 'swing' at the start (see **swing quavers** in the glossary).

+ Attend to the layout first. Get the instruments in the correct order and adjust the distance between the staves. Choose an appropriate number of bars per line and systems per page. Then enter title, stave labels, tempo, time and key signatures and make sure the clefs are correct.

+ Enter the details last. This includes dynamics, phrasing and articulation marks. Before you print off the individual parts make sure that you transpose them correctly for the instrument and that you sort out repeat marks and group multiple rests together. It might be an idea to save an extra version of the full score in case you make a mistake as you edit the parts.

Multitrack recording

Arrangement 2 can be recorded on a portastudio, an ADAT or a software audio system. The key feature of this arrangement is that it is worked up as a performance, possibly involving improvisation. Unlike the sequencing tasks, where the software makes it possible to experiment as you go along by copying, deleting, cutting and pasting, an arrangement made on a multitrack needs to be prepared in much more detail beforehand (although some of these computer operations can be carried out on a software recording system).

There are two basic approaches. The first is to overdub the instrumental tracks (either playing all the parts yourself or working with others). The following guidance may be helpful:

+ Work out the bare bones of the arrangement first, just as you would for a sequenced arrangement. This includes the chords, the structure, the instrumentation and the stylistic feel.

+ Write it out as a chord chart or lead-sheet so you and your players have a guide to work to. (These forms of notation are explained on page 96.)

+ Rehearse it live before attempting to record.

+ Record a click track of regular ticks or beeps as a reference for the other parts. Note that your choice of tempo will be one of the most crucial decisions you will have to make as, unlike sequencing, there is no way of altering this once recorded.

- As an alternative to a click track you could record a guide track (perhaps a rough version of the main melodic line). This could be prepared on a sequencer, giving you an opportunity to try out ideas and experiment with the tempo.

The second approach is to assemble and record the arrangement live in a studio. You can use close-miking or make a stereo ambient recording. You may find it helpful to record a backing track and overdub the solos later.

Much of the guidance above, about the need for preparation and providing the players with some form of notation, applies here although you should read the section below on improvisation.

Improvising

It is possible to arrive at a viable musical arrangement by working live with a band but you will have to maintain a fairly decisive role since you will be submitting the end result as your own work. It is not necessary to dictate every note but, on the other hand, it is not enough simply to set the band jamming and then disappear to the mixing desk.

Most importantly, you will need to have done some homework and be prepared to play through your ideas. You may take a chord chart, but players who do not read music notation may need to be talked through the arrangement. After the initial explanations you can guide the band, describing or demonstrating anything special that you want to achieve, for example:

- drum patterns and feels
- bass riffs, and the relationship between bass guitar and drums
- guitar strumming patterns, chord voicings, keyboard patterns
- fill ideas (rhythmic and melodic)
- chord spacings for live strings or wind.

Jazz musicians often use a head arrangement in which they all memorise the basic melody, its backing and the overall form the piece is to take. The performance consists of the head chorus interspersed with improvised solos and interludes. If you allow your players freedom to improvise solos, take care to keep them under control. This assignment must be no more than three minutes long and it is not an opportunity for the lead guitarist or saxophonist to indulge in an endless solo.

Improvising can often lead to the spontaneous creation of excellent ideas. If you feel the band is getting into a good groove let them continue and pick up on anything interesting at the end (it might be good practice to keep microphones running while you work). This is similar to a director working with actors.

On the other hand the band may be a little stiff and unwilling to experiment. Here you can try giving them a portion of the arrangement and letting them jam with it for a while.

Keep notes (a diary of rehearsals will do) so that you have a record of what took place. The quality of the final performance is not assessed, but your input is, so you must be able to identify your contribution as clearly as possible in your written commentary.

Final mix

The recordings should be mixed down into stereo on CD or mini-disc, taking account of balance, levels, panning, EQ and effects. Take great care with this final mix and try to avoid leaving it until the last minute. It is a very important part of the assessment.

You should also observe the general specification requirements in relation to recording, which state that you must be in sole charge of the mixing desk under the supervision of your teacher, and that you may not use a commercial studio for your coursework.

Commentary

You must provide a short written commentary detailing the resources used and your intentions. Not only is this assessed but it is also in many ways a key to the whole project: an opportunity for you to tell the examiner what you have done and what to listen for. Remember to include:

+ the title of the stimulus
+ details of instruments used and production processes employed
+ a short description of how you went about the task
+ an outline of how your arrangement differs from the original.

What the examiners look for

Your arrangements will be assessed against five criteria:

+ fidelity to the original, and quality of new ideas
+ handling of instruments and ensemble
+ use of technology
+ handling of timbre and texture
+ attention to detail.

Marks in the highest category go to work which shows attention to detail and which enhances the original while still remaining true to it. The arrangements will reveal secure handling of individual instruments, the entire ensemble and the technological resources used, with no (or very few) misjudgements.

Marks in the middle range are given to arrangements which are broadly faithful to the original and in which any additions, although possibly lacking refinement in places, do not detract from the overall quality. The work will show that resources have been used competently, though not always imaginatively, and the technical presentation will be clear, even if lacking in detail.

Marks in the lower ranges will go to work in which there is extensive carelessness or little creative input. There will be significant errors or misjudgements in the use of the resources and poor presentation is likely to have compromised the end result.

Listening and Analysing (AS)

In this section, we'll be looking at the kind of things you need to know to complete the two-hour written exam at the end of your AS course. As you can see from the title of the exam you will need two sets of skills. You will need to be able to listen clearly and analyse what you hear in response to the questions.

The questions on this paper relate to two areas of study – *The Development of Music Technology* and *Popular Music and Jazz*. They will be a mixture of multiple-choice questions and short-answer questions that often need just a few words or sentences in response, plus a final essay question where you will need to write in continuous prose in a logical way. In this last question, you will be marked on spelling, grammar and clarity as well as your listening and analysising skills.

For the exam you will have a CD with eight extracts from recordings of popular music or jazz and two complete songs. You can listen (on headphones) to the extracts as often as you wish within the overall time allowed. You have to answer all of the questions on the first eight extracts and then answer either question 9 or question 10 (the essay questions).

Helpful practice material for the listening tests is given in *AS/A2 Listening Tests for Music Technology* by Andy Collyer, Rhinegold Publishing Ltd, ISBN 1-904226-45-0. Workbook and Audio CD, each available separately. In addition, specimen and past papers are available from Edexcel.

For this exam paper, you will need to demonstrate the ability to:

+ identify recording techniques and effects
+ identify musical styles and put music into a historical context
+ use a musical and technological vocabulary
+ analyse unfamiliar music
+ compare pieces of music
+ recognise and understand musical elements such as rhythm, melody, harmony and form
+ read standard staff notation.

This may seem like a lot to ask when you see it in a list like this but after two and a half term's preparation and a lot of practical experience in coursework, you will have a solid base of technological knowledge and vocabulary on which to build. Your arranging coursework and the analysis of your classical piece for sequencing or recording will help you with the musical vocabulary.

Technological elements

You will be asked to describe various ways in which technology has been used to create a specific sound. This could include:

+ recording and mixing techniques or methods (multi-tracked studio recording, live studio recording, live location recording, mic placement, the use of ambient or spot-mic techniques, double-tracking, use of the stereo spectrum etc)
+ use of specific effects and dynamics processors (reverb, echo, **distortion**, **chorus**, **flange**, EQ, **pitch shift**, ADT, compressors, **gates** etc)
+ use of electronic instruments (eg guitars, synth drums and drum machines, electric pianos, organs, synthesisers, samplers and perhaps older electronic instruments).

This is where your practical work will help you. Hopefully you will have explored your school's studio and experimented with mic placement, microphone types and effects units. If you can remember what your experiments sounded like, you only have to compare what you hear on the exam CD with what you created yourself.

For example you will undoubtedly have had problems with distortion at some point. You know what distortion sounds like and can identify it in a recording. Similarly, you may have applied timed delay to a guitar track, chorus to a vocal line, beefed up a bass with EQ, panned a drum kit or compressed vocals. If you can remember what all these things sound like, you have the key to this element of the exam – sonic memory!

Listening to a wide range of music is equally important. Always read the CD booklet. This will often tell you what instruments have been used (particularly in older recordings). If you hear unusual instruments like a mellotron, vocoder or talkbox (see *left*) try to remember the characteristics of that particular sound.

Terminology

You should use appropriate terminology. For example:

+ If you need to write about preventing popping, use the term 'pop shield' rather than describing a pair of tights on a coathanger or calling it a muffler.

+ Describe effects specifically, using terms like 'large-hall reverb' or 'small-room reverb' rather than just reverb.

+ You won't be required to refer to specific frequency bands but phrases such as 'I would cut some of the low-mid frequencies' would be expected.

+ If you are asked to comment on the quality of a recording, try to be specific. So rather than saying it sounds 'dull and boomy' try to describe precisely what causes these impressions. It might be because of a 'limited frequency range', 'poor separation of instruments' and 'excessive use of large-hall reverberation on the bass guitar'.

+ If you are asked to describe production values or sampled sounds that have no specific terminology, try to be as accurate and as descriptive as possible. For instance: 'This is a warm and spacious mix that allows the voice to cut through clearly', or 'The sample that sounds like a spade being dragged across a paving stone'.

The mellotron is a keyboard instrument that was popular in the 1970s. When you press a key a tape loop of sounds such as strings, choirs or horn sections is engaged with a tape playback head. Its distinctive sound is used to effect on *Watcher of the Skies* and other tracks from Genesis' album *Foxtrot*. Sampled mellotron sounds have made a comeback recently.

The vocoder is a device that modulates a signal from a mic with a signal from another source (often a keyboard) allowing musical notes to sound like speech. Hear it on The Electric Light Orchestra's *Mr Blue Sky* from *The Light Years – The Very Best of ELO*. This sound came back into use recently in dance music. Listen to the title track of Madonna's album *Music*.

The talkbox sends the output from a guitar amp through a box that has a tube leading to the performer's mouth which can be used to modify the sound, which is then picked up by a mic. Hear it on the track *Do You Feel Like I Do?* from Peter Frampton's album *Frampton Comes Alive*. Fast forward to about seven minutes into the track if you want to avoid the typically indulgent 1970s solos!

? **Private study**

Listen to *One Day* from Björk's album *Debut* and then answer the following questions.

1. What effect has been used on Björk's spoken vocal in the intro?

2. Describe the filtering of the opening arpeggiated sample.

3. Describe the panning of the metallic-sounding sample.

4. What effect has been used on Björk's sung vocal?

Musical elements

You will be asked to identify and comment on various musical elements including:

✦ rhythmic and melodic structures
✦ recognition of major keys, minor keys and chord progressions
✦ form and structure
✦ identifying musical instruments and ensembles
✦ performance qualities (specific instrumental techniques and interpretative skills).

The skills and vocabulary you have learned through arranging will come into play for this element. You will have been taught about structure and form and will have learned something about different instruments, ensembles and textures. Your music-reading skills should now be consolidated.

Again, appropriate terminology should be used. For example:

✦ When describing rhythmic or melodic devices, try to use terms such as **syncopation**, **ostinato**, sequence, **riff**, tempo, bpm etc (remember to take a watch into the exam – you can count the number of beats in 15 seconds and multiply by four for a fairly accurate bpm).

✦ When identifying chords in pop music, it is preferable to use letter notation (such as F^7 or Cm) rather than Roman numerals (such as I or IV).

✦ When describing form in pop music, use terms such as intro, verse 1, bridge, chorus, verse 2, bridge, chorus, instrumental, bridge, chorus to fade, etc, rather than letters (such as ABA^1).

✦ You should be able to recognise and name prominent pop and jazz instruments (guitar, bass, various types of keyboard, drums, trumpet, trombone, sax, flute etc) and ensembles (string section, horn section, jazz combo, string quartet etc).

✦ You should be able to use terms such as staccato, pizzicato, **muted**, **pitch bend**, **legato**, swing quavers and **rubato**, and to describe 'a breathy vocal', 'the use of dynamic contrasts', etc.

You will be asked about time signatures. Mostly you will hear simple time (2/4, 3/4, 4/4) in which each beat divides into two quavers (or eighth-notes). However, you may encounter compound time (6/8, 9/8, 12/8) in which each beat divides into three. If you can count '1–and 2–and' (etc) the beat is simple. If the feel is '1–and–a 2–and–a' (etc) the beat will be compound. You may also be asked about changing time signatures. The easiest and most effective way to work these out is to feel where the strong beats are and count the gaps on your fingers!

In dealing with rhythms, the first thing to do is to establish where the beat is and what it is. Having established that it is 4/4, for example, subdivide the beat into quavers, or semiquavers if necessary, and work out how the rhythm you are trying to establish fits. Think in terms of a drum edit page (see *right*), draw a grid and then work out the time values.

When trying to identify the form or structure of a piece of music, listen for phrase lengths, repeated ideas and cadences. These will help you to determine when sections begin and end.

A rhythm in drum edit:

The same rhythm in notation:

With chords, you have to be able to hear the root note (which may or may not be the bottom note if inversions are being used) and relate it to the tonic, or key note. If you can hum the keynote and the root of the chord you wish to identify, all you need to do is hum up the scale to work out its number. You are unlikely to be asked about chords other than I, II, IV, V and VI and these are quite easy to recognise with a little practice.

You can work out the pitch of melodies in a similar way. Providing you can hum up and down the scale, you should be able to decide on the pitches required – the example left shows the actual melody in larger notes with the scale steps between these indicated by small noteheads.

There will be some questions that require you to read staff notation in order to identify the correct melody or rhythm that you hear. You may be asked to add a note, rest or **accidental** to a short written phrase in order to make it correct.

Private study

Listen to *This Year's Love* from David Gray's CD *White Ladder* and then answer the following questions.

1. Is the time signature 4/4, 3/4, 6/8 or 9/4?

2. Fill in the missing chords for bars 2–8 of the track using *either* letters *or* numbers. The key is A♭ major and the chord in bar 1 is shown. Note that there are two chords in bar 8.

Bar	1	2	3	4	5	6	7	8
Chord	D♭							
	IV							

3. This track includes a piano and voice. What other instruments can be heard?

4. All of the pitches from the first vocal phrase are shown *left*. Rearrange them in the correct order:

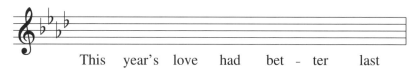

Style and context

This is possibly the most difficult area to answer questions on as it relies on you having listened to a wide range of recordings in different genres throughout your AS and A2 courses. You'll need to be able to comment on the following areas:

✦ the period when the extract was recorded or written (these may not be the same) and some general background to that period

✦ the style or genre of the music and how it relates to other music of a similar kind

✦ how this kind of music developed, the sort of people who made it and the context in which it was recorded.

A lot of the information you need to identify the period of the recording of an extract will be revealed by the technology used.

If you hear a monophonic synthesiser, this will place the recording sometime after the mid 1960s. If the synthesiser is polyphonic, the date will be sometime after the mid to late 1970s. If you hear sampling, the date will be from about 1980 onwards. Listen carefully to synth sounds from different decades and remember how fashions changed. You can do the same with guitar timbres. As various effects pedals became available and were made popular, the sounds guitarists chose to use changed and developed.

If the recording is in mono, that will date it to some time before 1954 when the first stereo tapes were released to the public. Recordings from the first half of the century are also likely to have a narrow range of frequencies, poor balance and some distortion due to the quality of mics and limited recording technology.

The positioning of sounds in the stereo spectrum can also help to date a recording. In the early days of stereo, engineers and producers were much more extreme than they are today where sounds are equally balanced around the centre. The 1960s are often characterised by extreme panning, such as the drums all to the left and the lead vocals to the right. The late 1960s and early 1970s recordings, especially in the field of progressive rock, often had sounds moving through the stereo field from speaker to speaker.

Beware of music in the last decade or so that has been deliberately recorded badly or roughly (what is known as **lo-fi**).

So you can see how the technology available and the way it is used can help you to place a recording historically. In terms of dating the song and establishing its genre or style, things are a little less cut and dried, but we have covered this in detail in the chapter on popular music and jazz (starting on page 25).

See http://www.digitalcentury.com/encyclo/update/audiohd.html

Monophonic synths: listen to *The Six Wives of Henry VIII* by Rick Wakeman (1973) to hear typical Moog sounds of the period.

Polyphonic synths: listen to *Songs in the Key of Life* by Stevie Wonder for some early polyphonic synth sounds.

Sampling: listen to *Peter Gabriel 4* for some very creative use of the Fairlight CMI.

Mono recording: listen to *Hey Now* by Ray Charles (it's on the June 2001 exam paper – your teacher should have a copy).

Stereo: extreme panning can be heard on the Beatles' CD *Revolver*. Virtually anything from the 1970s by Tangerine Dream will reveal shifting panning.

Multiple-choice questions

In these questions, you will generally be asked to choose from four answers. If you are not sure of the answer you can normally narrow down your choice by a process of elimination. There may be one obvious wrong answer, a red herring. That will leave you with three, two of which are 'probables'. Let's look at an example. Listen to the opening of *Lost Ones* from *The Miseducation of Lauryn Hill*. A question might read as follows:

The drum sample on this recording could best be described as:

(a) 45 bpm   (b) syncopated   (c) polyrhythmic   (d) ethnic

The red herring is answer (a) as the music is clearly faster than this. The next answer to discount would be (d) as the beat has little ethnic influence and is very clearly urban in feel. This leaves you with syncopated and polyrhythmic. Providing you have a clear understanding of at least one of these terms you should be able to recognise either that the loop is syncopated – or that it is clearly not polyrhythmic. Either way, you have arrived at the correct answer by looking logically at the options.

? Private study

Listen to *Ex-Factor*, the second track on the Lauryn Hill CD, and answer the following questions.

1. Which tuned-percussion instrument is featured on this track?

    (a) snare drum   (b) wind chimes   (c) timpani   (d) bass drum

2. Which of the following best describes the first chord of the two-bar pattern?

    (a) dominant 7th   (b) minor 7th   (c) flattened tonic   (d) major

3. Which of the following describes the treatment of the vocals?

    (a) flanged   (b) chorused   (c) sampled   (d) multitracked

Comparison questions

There will be a question where you will be asked to compare two recordings of the same song. These comparisons could be stylistic, technological, structural, textural or performance-based.

The two versions of the song will be in different styles and will feature different performance qualities. You will have to identify elements that make the two extracts different. These may include:

✦ the feel or the groove (funky, mellow, driving rock, dance, agitated, ballad, syncopated, smooth etc)

✦ the style of singing or playing (expressive, deadpan, soulful, simple, complex, technically demanding etc)

✦ the type of instruments used (acoustic as opposed to electric, played live as opposed to electronically generated etc).

There will undoubtedly be technological differences between the two, which may include:

✦ general clarity (a recording from the 1940s and a cover version of the same song made in the 1990s would have a marked difference in frequency range or there may be noise or distortion in older recordings, for example)

✦ use of stereo field, effects and relative levels in the mix

✦ use of instruments (some of which may not even have been invented when the original version was recorded).

The structure of the extracts may be the same, completely different or show only subtle differences. The difference could be as simple as adding an extra four bars to the intro or it could be as noticeable as starting with a chorus rather than a verse. Changes of time signature, from a straight 4/4 to 12/8 for example, should be noted as a change in the structure.

In terms of texture, or the combination of instruments and how they contribute to the overall sound, the differences may be subtle or conspicuous. One version may be guitar based, the other working through keyboards, one may have a thinner texture (less going on) than the other. As always, make sure you use the correct musical terminology.

Private study

Listen to recordings of *Here, There and Everywhere* by the Beatles on their CD *Revolver* and by Celine Dion on George Martin's CD *In My Life* and then answer the following questions.

1. Name three differences in instrumentation and texture between the two versions.

2. Describe the different ways in which the vocals have been recorded and mixed in each version.

3. What are the stylistic elements that set these two recordings apart?

4. Compare the vocal interpretation in each version.

Try to compare as many cover versions with original recordings as you can find. Some will be substantially different while others will be little changed. Here are some ideas to start you off:

Always on my Mind – Elvis Presley / The Pet Shop Boys
American Pie – Don McLean / Madonna
Eternal Flame – The Bangles / Atomic Kitten
How Deep is your Love – The Beegees / Take That
Lucy in the Sky with Diamonds – The Beatles / Elton John
She – Charles Aznavour / Elvis Costello
There She Goes – The La's / Sixpence None the Richer
Walk On By – Dionne Warwick / Gabrielle

Essay question

The format of this question will remain basically the same from year to year. The elements you will be asked to consider are:

+ style and genre
+ structure and form
+ instrumentation and texture
+ performance quality and interpretation
+ technology.

We have covered all of these issues in previous sections.

You should stick to the headings which are given to you in the paper to help you work your way logically and clearly through the essay (it will also help the examiner to mark more easily and put him or her in a better mood).

You will have a choice of two pieces of music to write about. It's not always a good idea to pick the recording that you know or the song by one of your favourite bands. You can often hear and identify more in an unfamiliar recording than in something that you know well. You should also bear in mind that this is not the place to voice your opinions about good and bad music – try to be objective and state facts backed up with evidence.

Your use of language, grammar and spelling will be assessed in this essay question, so make sure you use appropriate vocabulary and proper sentence structures, and spell as accurately as you can. Never make bullet point lists. This will certainly lose you valuable marks.

? Private study

Listen to a selection of the recordings listed below and for each write an analysis of 200–250 words in continuous prose, using the following beginnings for paragraphs:

✦ The style of the song … and then describe the genre and how it relates to other music.

✦ The structure … and then describe the melodic, rhythmic, harmonic and structural elements.

✦ The instrumentation and texture … and then describe the instruments, how they are used and their effect on the overall sound.

✦ The performances … and then describe and evaluate the performances in terms of fluency and communication.

✦ The technology … and then describe and evaluate the uses of technology and their effectiveness.

Money for Nothing by Dire Straits on the CD *Money for Nothing*
Maxine by Donald Fagen on the CD *The Nightfly*
Beethoven (I Love To Listen To) by Eurythmics on the CD *Savage*
The Logical Song by Supertramp on the CD *Breakfast in America*
Common People by Pulp on the CD *Different Class*
The Sea by Morcheeba on the CD *Big Calm*
Tender by Blur on the CD *13*

Exam technique

You will be given time to make sure the CD and the equipment you are playing it on are working. Make sure that you have the headphone-level set comfortably but loud enough for you to hear subtleties in the recordings.

In the first eight questions, the answers can be short sentences or single words. Don't waste time writing paragraphs when they are not required.

Each question will tell you how many marks you can score. If a question is worth four marks, make sure you say *at least* four different things to get all the marks. Repeating a point, even if you use different words, will not gain a mark.

Always use technological and musical words and phrases accurately. Write neatly in dark ink: your examiner will be more kindly disposed to you if you do!

Time yourself carefully. Remember that the essay question is worth 20 marks, while the first eight questions carry only ten marks each. This means that you must allow roughly double the time for the last question. If you are really struggling with a part of a question worth only one or two marks, carry on with the rest and come back to it at the end if you have time.

Sequencing, Recording and Producing (A2)

Requirements

This section of A2 Music Technology brings together sequencing, recording and production skills in a project which has three parts and that builds on the skills you developed in the AS course. You will be required to produce three recordings, as outlined below.

Recording 1

A multitrack digital recording of a piece of music using a balanced mixture of close-mic and DI techniques. It must involve the use of **at least eight (but no more than 16) live tracks**. No sequenced tracks may be included – all the material must be played by live musicians. The recording should be between three and five minutes in length. It must involve the use of effects processing and the management of dynamics. You are required to use overdubbing and it is expected that you will spend considerable time working on a creative mixdown to stereo after the recording sessions.

Note that the minimum is eight tracks, not four (as was stated in Edexcel's original specification). This doesn't necessarily mean eight performers. For instance, you might devote four tracks to drums (snare, bass and a stereo pair overhead), and the other four to vocals, saxophone, bass and keyboards.

You are not allowed to use one of your own compositions for this project. The music, which may be purely instrumental if you wish, must be a piece that is commercially available (ie it must exist in recorded and/or written forms, or form part of a commercially-available repertoire).

Recording 2

A sequenced MIDI backing of a song, making use of at least six instrumental tracks (for A2, a keyboard part counts as only one instrument). **In addition** the sequence must include a guide MIDI melody line voiced to a suitable instrumental timbre.

Note that the use of commercially produced MIDI tracks or auto-arrange software is not permitted.

The song should be two to three minutes long. It will probably be in a pop or jazz style, in which case it is expected that you will work from a lead-sheet (or even by ear) and do at least some of the arranging yourself. When choosing the song you need to bear in mind that for the third part of this paper you have to add a live vocal part to your recording of the backing. You should therefore choose a song that is suitable for the singer(s) you intend to use.

The backing should contain enough material to provide ample melodic, harmonic and rhythmic interest and contrast. For a good mark you will be expected to spend time and effort in refining the work – editing individual notes, attack and dynamics to achieve style and phrasing, and using tempo, timbre, balance and panning to create musical results. The entire backing (with guide melody) must then be recorded to stereo. You are not required to produce a score of your sequenced backing.

Recording 3

A studio recording that combines the prepared sequenced backing material of Recording 2 with **between two and four live audio tracks**. One of these **must be a vocal track** in which the melody that you laid down as a guide part in your sequence is *replaced* by a sung performance. The final recording must be mixed down to stereo and may require the use of effects processing.

Your submission must **not** include the original synthesised guide part for the vocalist. Your singer(s) may need this part routed to their foldback mix, but you must ensure that the track is muted in your final mix. You can, if you wish, use a similar technique for any live instrumental part(s). For instance you might include a synthesised trumpet part in the original sequenced backing, but replace it with a live trumpet in the recording. Instrumentalists are far less likely to want to play to a guide part of this sort since it can be very distracting, but in all such cases the guide track must not duplicate the live track in the final recording.

Coursework submission

The final mix of all three recordings must be submitted on CD or mini-disc. You must also submit a floppy disk containing the sequenced backing track saved in type 1 MIDI file format **and** in the proprietary format of the sequencing package you used (eg Cubase, Logic, Cakewalk etc). You will also need to submit the source material (lead-sheet, score or recording) from which you developed the sequenced backing tracks.

All these items must be sent to the examiner by 15 May in your A2 examination year, along with log sheets for each of the three components, track sheets and equipment lists. Note that Edexcel provides a 'submission booklet' for all the documentation, but it is essential that you keep your own records as the work progresses. This will then make the form-filling much easier!

You will be fulfilling the role of both engineer and producer in this unit. As recording engineer you will be using the tools of the studio to make the best quality recordings you can. As producer you will be overseeing the creative process and using studio techniques to develop and enhance your work. It is fair to suggest that as you move from AS to A2 and your skills develop, you will move from basic engineering to true production. As such you may wish to re-read earlier parts of this guide as and when you feel you need to, according to the techniques you wish to explore and the tasks you have to undertake.

This substantial project needs to be started as early as possible in the course. Each of the three recordings attracts an equal mark weighting and the examiners will expect the work to have been through a long process of refinement and to show imagination, musicality and accuracy. To achieve high marks your recordings will need to impress with their quality and impact. You will need to show secure handling of the musical and technical resources available, and skills in arranging, sequencing and recording that result in outstanding recorded performances.

Composing

Requirements

You have to complete two tasks:

1. A composition in any style or form, to a brief chosen by you or your teacher. This can be composed at any time during the course (even during your AS year).

2. A composition to a brief set by Edexcel and sent out at the start of the spring term. There will be a choice of briefs relating to Area of Study 4a (*Words and Music*) and 4b (*Music and the Moving Image*). You will already have chosen one of these Areas of Study and started looking at the set works in preparation for the written exam and it is expected that you will choose the same one for your composition.

The two compositions must each be about three minutes in length and add up to six minutes in total, and each must be composed for at least four tracks/instruments/voices. They do not have to be contrasting. For example if you opt for a film-music brief for Composition 2 you can still choose film music for Composition 1.

The following items must be sent to the examiner by 15 May in your A2 examination year:

+ a recording of each piece on CD or mini-disc (**not** on the same disc you used for Sequencing, Recording and Producing)
+ a computer-originated score of each piece
+ a written commentary about each piece (Edexcel provides a form for this).

Introduction

Edexcel requires you to use technology as a resource in your compositions. Technology is not something which composers add on – throughout history it has played a part in shaping the way they actually think about music. Here are some examples.

+ From 1750 onwards piano makers developed a new hammer system called the *escapement action*. This allowed the hammer to bounce back from the string much more efficiently so that notes could be repeated quickly and chords could sound more percussive. Beethoven took a great interest in this and used this new capability extensively. Many of his piano sonatas feature techniques which would not have been possible on earlier instruments – for example the *Appassionata* sonata with its fast repeated notes in the bass and loud, thick-textured chords.

+ The invention of the *flat-disc gramophone* in 1887 by Emile Berliner provided a commercial outlet for composers outside the dance hall and concert hall, but early records could store only a few minutes of music. Songs with many repeated verses and extended solos were out of the question and song writers had to adapt to the new medium. The 32-bar song, with its concise AABA structure, became the standard form, probably helped by the fact that there was enough space on one side of a record to get through 32 bars twice at a quick dance tempo.

+ The development of multitrack recording during the 1960s changed the entire recording process. Instead of gathering all the performers together and recording the song in one take, composers could build up parts one at a time and mix them at the end. This enabled them to record a basic structure (the backing track) leaving time later to experiment with the other layers. It also enabled a small number of musicians (or a solo musician) to play multiple parts by overdubbing.

+ When the drum machine came on to the market in the early 1980s, closely followed by the sequencer and MIDI, it was possible to do without a live performer. Because sequenced music can seem mechanical it has a unique sound, which is most obvious in the work of 1980s electro-rock bands like Human League and OMD. Parts that would be unplayable by human hands can be played by the machine. Moreover the keyboard has become the standard instrument for entering MIDI data and so composers tend to write for all instruments (including bass, strings and brass) using keyboard finger patterns. The sound of MIDI instrumentation is therefore often very different to that made by a band or an ensemble of live players.

Composing with technology today

As the above examples show, each technological advance has allowed composers to find new ways of controlling elements like form, texture, rhythm and timbre. We are in a fortunate position today because equipment is not only more sophisticated but also cheaper than ever. Many studio features, which may have cost thousands of pounds 20 years ago, can now be purchased as software on a CD-ROM or downloaded from the Internet.

But what makes technology special for the composer is that it opens up an entirely new range of compositional techniques.

Sequencing Sequencing makes it possible to hear music while you are composing it. You can use the mouse to manipulate the building blocks of a composition from individual notes and bars to tracks and phrases, and even entire sections. You can choose to do this in real time (with the sequence running) or in step time (by carrying out the operations one at a time with the sequence stopped). The most common operations are:

+ cutting and pasting ideas from one part to another
+ copying and repeating bars, tracks or sections
+ merging tracks
+ inserting new ideas
+ looping sections so you can hear them repeated
+ soloing a track so you can hear it on its own.

These can all be done on the main display, usually referred to as the arrange window. Here you can try out different versions of a piece, saving each one separately (using the save-as function) and then choosing your favourite or editing together all the best bits.

Sequencing programs also allow you very fine control over the performance details:

- correcting wrong notes
- quantising rhythms
- editing syncopation and adjusting the feel or groove of a track
- editing articulation, accents and phrasing
- setting volume, pan, pitch bend (known as 'control changes')
- changing instruments (known as 'program changes')
- automating faders and effects.

When using the sequencer as a composition tool there are a number of things you will need to watch out for.

- Cut-and-paste is a very useful function but try to avoid copying sections end on end just to make up the length – the ear quickly gets bored with identical repeats.

- Try not to get hypnotised by looped samples and riffs – they may seem interesting while you are experimenting with them but again be careful not to overdo the repetition.

- The design of the computer track display makes it very easy to compose all your music in four-bar patterns. Too many of these will lend a square and predictable feel to the music.

- With so many GM sounds to choose from it is tempting to keep adding timbres. Not only is this tiring to listen to, but new sounds are no substitute for interesting content.

- Remember that computers can crash. Always save your work as you go along and always back it up on to a separate disk.

Timbre

Staff notation is in many ways an imperfect method for recording the details of a composition. The information it conveys about note lengths and pitches is only relative and there is no system or set of symbols for timbre except in special cases such as specifying organ stops, or the use of a mute, or when a string player is required to use a particular string for its special tone colour. However technology has revolutionised the way composers control timbre.

The range of GM sounds includes all standard instruments of the orchestra, a range of keyboard instruments, tuned and untuned percussion, and instruments from around the world, as well as synthesised instruments and pads. Most synthesisers and computer sound cards will allow you to edit these timbres by changing the envelope or waveform, by filtering or detuning, or by adding low-frequency oscillation or mixing in other timbres. It is also possible to purchase specialist modules containing, for example, dance sounds, Asian instruments and electric guitar samples.

Additional control is possible using effects and processors. It is standard practice for studio engineers to use these to improve the quality of the recorded sound in the production process by removing unwanted noise or by equalising to adjust tone quality. However, many instrumental timbres result from effects that are applied directly to the instrument. One of the simplest examples of this is the use of electric guitar outboards like distortion pedals, although it is not unusual today for guitarists to have an entire rack of units.

GM timbres often include built-in effects such as pianos with reverberation, strings with chorus, bass guitars with flanging, and drums with delay. These can usually be edited so that when you select an instrument is it also possible to select its effect's reverberation time, depth of chorus and so on. Alternatively a particular instrumental track can have effects added by passing it through a unit.

Effects units can also be used to transform a timbre quite radically. It is currently fashionable in UK garage music to process the vocal track using vocoders, harmonisers or ring modulators and many sound installations in art galleries feature one sound being slowly transformed into another over a period of time, for example running water gradually changing into insects buzzing and back again in a long loop.

Multitracking and mixing

Multitrack recorders, whether tape, digital or computer-based, can allow you to construct textures and layers quite easily.

Overdubbing is a common and popular recording technique; parts can be doubled or built up to create a much thicker sound and instruments can play more than one part.

On a computer sequencer the texture is easy to manipulate because the track display shows how the various tracks are combined in the form of an interactive diagram: the mouse can be used to drag and drop them from one part of the composition to another. Some composers prefer to use this feature to record all their basic ideas first, and then drag and copy them into the arrangement in different combinations until they are satisfied with the result. Others prefer to start with a single track and build up from there.

Printing

Printing technology, like recording technology, is now available at a fraction of the price it was 20 years ago. Music can be entered on most scorewriting packages by playing it on a keyboard in real time, or by entering the notes and symbols one at a time with the mouse. It is also possible to load a performance from disk, recorded on another system, in the form of a MIDI file.

Note that while scorewriting software can help you produce a well-presented score, this must not be your *only* use of technology in the compositions. The music itself must use technology in an integrated way.

Once you have entered the basic performance details there are three main stages in the preparation of a professional-looking score. First, you need to get the layout right. Instruments need to be in the correct order (eg woodwind at the top, strings at the bottom) and lyrics need to be aligned correctly below the vocal parts. Although the computer will usually work out things like margins automatically you will have to choose an appropriate number of bars per line. Four or five is usual but you may have to fiddle around with the font size. Try to avoid ending up with one bar per line and staves full of rests otherwise the score will run to a ridiculous number of pages. Next you need to check all the rudiments; time and key signatures, accidentals, rests and so on. Lastly you enter the details – dynamics, phrasing, articulation marks.

If you do not read music, scorewriting packages can be quite hard work as there is so much editing which requires a knowledge of music theory (see the section starting on page 68). But there is no doubt that they offer a wide range of labour-saving operations like extracting parts for individual players, transposing and perhaps even checking for notes that are out of the instrument's range.

On older synthesisers instrumental sounds, including orchestral instruments, had to be artificially created by programming. The sampler, however, takes a digital snapshot of a sound so the real thing can be saved and replayed. Many of the GM timbres on a synthesiser or sound card are digitally encoded from samples so acoustic instruments like pianos, violins, woodwind and brass are reproduced with more accuracy. This development has had the interesting side effect of making the older analogue sounds rather retro and fashionable.

Sampling

A completely new technique of composing has grown up around sampling, in which a composer samples portions of other composers' music and reworks them to create an entirely new piece. This may involve drum patterns (known as 'drum loops'), riffs or more extended melodies and phrases. The guitar riffs of Jimmy Page of Led Zeppelin, and the drum-and-bass patterns of veteran soul singer James Brown are among the most frequently sampled. There are also a great many commercial CDs containing samples and these are sometimes given away free with music technology journals – it is also possible to download them from the internet.

For samples try www.samplearena.com

Sampling can be quite tricky as it involves making a recording of the original and then trimming it to the length required. This has done so as to create a seamless join when the sample is looped and played end on end. Once a sample has been created it can be saved as a **wav file** and imported into a sequencing program. In order to combine samples in different keys or with different bpm you may have to transpose or stretch one of them. Sampling software usually includes a sample calculator and a transform function.

Anyone who depends on samples should check the copyright position because the borrowed ideas are actually someone else's property. Any samples from other people's music in your A2 compositions must be identified in your commentary on the work.

The Internet

The existence of the Internet has enabled musicians to explore new ways in which their work can be distributed. Scores, arrangements, commercial CDs, samples and pop videos can now all be downloaded from the Internet – often as compressed MP3 files which are more compact than wav files. Many artists now release their material on a website, sometimes giving fans an opportunity to download, remix and then send it back.

Interesting websites for composers include http://www.peoplesound.com and http://www.taxi.com

In addition, free software (including trial versions) and technical manuals can be downloaded – the websites of most of the major manufacturers of software and equipment will provide you with useful links.

For free software and trials try http://www.prosoniq.com

The World Wide Web can also be a very useful research tool for looking-up CD reviews, exploring aspects of world music and so on, but it needs to be used with caution. Printed publications are normally checked very carefully for accuracy by specialist editors, expert advisors and professional proof-readers before publication. Websites, on the other hand, can be launched by anyone, whether they have expertise in their subject or not, and some may offer information which is confused, naive, incomplete or sometimes even totally wrong.

Planning

Compositions need planning. The arrangements which you made for your AS exam will have provided useful experience and you will also have analysed music in the areas of study. However you may find the following general guidance helpful. Individual styles of music are covered in more detail later in the chapter.

Melody   When composing a melody think about its structure:

+ How many bars per phrase? How many bars per verse?

+ How is variety achieved? Which phrases are repeated? How do the verse and chorus melodies differ?

+ What is the shape of the melody? Does it rise, does it fall or is it more like a chant?

+ Is there a memorable hook?

Harmony   The harmony often determines both the mood and structure of a song – whether it is in the major or minor, if it sounds jazzy, how the middle eight contrasts and so on. It may help to buy a chord dictionary to learn how chords are played and structured. Also, analyse songs (there are plenty in the areas of study) to see how other composers use harmony.

+ How many chords per phrase/verse? How often do they change? How often is the pattern repeated?

+ How do the chords follow one another? Is there a pattern? How do they sound if they are inverted or strummed differently?

+ Are there any changes of key? Are they gradual or abrupt?

+ How is dissonance used? Are there any 7th or 9th chords? Are there dissonances in the melody and/or the backing?

Rhythm   Rhythm plays a crucial role in determining style. Dance music is very syncopated, jazz often has a swing feel, reggae chords are played on the off-beat. Try some of these exercises:

+ Clap a rhythm, then try repeating it in a different style.

+ Play a well-known melody in a different rhythm.

+ Take a well-known riff and try writing down the rhythm.

+ Use the rhythm of drum tracks and percussion parts as the basis for bass riffs and chordal backings.

Timbre   Before you start to compose have a think about the overall sound quality you want your piece to have:

+ What instruments will you use? Will there be any backing vocals, strings etc?

+ How will you introduce variety? There needs to be some 'air' in the arrangement. If all the instruments are playing all the time the texture will tend to be dull.

+ Do you want a lo-fi or hi-fi production? What effects might you need?

Most students tend to start their pieces with an idea for a tune, a riff or a chord pattern. However thought given to structure at an early stage will help to give the song a clear sense of direction:

♦ Where will the repeats go? Will there be a middle section or an instrumental solo?

♦ Some pieces are structured around texture. Think about how these might be arranged.

♦ Listen to other songs. What are the memorable landmarks? Is there an introduction or a climax?

Lastly, make sure you take advantage of all that technology has to offer. Try out different arrangements and mixes, save them and choose the best for the examination.

Composition briefs

The brief for Composition 1, which can be in any style, is chosen by you or your teacher, while the brief for Composition 2 is set by Edexcel. In this section we will look at the types of brief that may be set and at other compositional styles and ideas which are suited to technology and which you might consider for your own brief.

Music for film and TV

This is not only a very popular topic for free composition, but also one of the area of study composition briefs. First, a general point about composing for film. You will almost always be working to a set timing. Within this overall time there may be places where a musical effect coincides exactly with the visual images – called 'sync points'. It is helpful to draw these out, either on a plain sheet or on a score, so you know how much music you need to compose. Start with the important passages first then decide how you want to build up to them or prepare for the next sync point. If you are working on a computer sequencer the program will work out the relationship between the number of bars, tempo and duration and you will be able to enter the tracks you need on the track display and align them according to the timings.

A good book on film composition technique is the **Complete Guide to Film Scoring** by Richard Davis. *Berklee Press*, 2000. ISBN: 0-634-00636-3.

In a professional editing suite it is usual to record a time code, often using a system called **SMPTE**. This is an electronic clock signal divided into hours, minutes, seconds and frames (in Britain 25 frames per second on video). Once recorded on to a track on each recording machine it will keep sound and video (and devices such as drum machines and sequencers) locked together. Fast winding the video to a particular spot will cause synchronised machines to move to the same spot. The code is used as a reference point. For example if you want the music to start when a car door slams you need to know the code for that particular moment. If you are using a computer sequencer you can use the mouse to drag your tracks to that point in the timecode and it is usually possible to change the ruler so it displays SMPTE rather than bar number.

SMTPE is an acronym (prounced 'simpty') for the Society of Motion Picture and Television Engineers – the body that developed this time code.

Another thing to bear in mind is the differing scale of TV and film music. Material written for television use tends to employ fewer instruments, partly because budgets are smaller but also because the sound of a large orchestra can sound tinny on television loud-speakers and 'out of scale' on a small screen.

Film and television music can be submitted in a variety of ways.

Title themes

Edexcel's sample questions include a brief for composing the titles for an historical drama with a love story, set in the English civil war of the 17th century. You are required to compose two themes: opening titles to portray the conflict and end-credits to reflect the love story. Another brief is a theme for a television documentary about a space station. The theme, in this case, must be composed using abstract electronic timbres.

Titles are intended to get the viewer in the right mood and also act as an accompaniment to the credits. The music for the end-credits is often much longer, since there are more screens of text to get through, and the musical ideas may be a variation of the opening, especially if the drama calls for a happy or sad ending.

Titles tend to rely on musical clichés such as rock music or lots of percussion and brass instruments for action, a romantic melody for love stories, fanfares and marches for sport. The English civil war theme mentioned above, could include some period music (which you would need to research) and something to suggest war (composers often find a military-sounding snare drum part very useful for this). The musical style would have to be softened to depict the love story (perhaps by slowing the tempo or using strings). One very professional approach would be to use the same theme for the titles *and* the end, dressed up and arranged as a warlike march to start and as a gentle ballad to finish. In fact, a useful exercise for the film composer is to take a well-known melody and see how many ways it can be transformed into a different feel or mood.

Underscore

An underscore is the music played during the film or television programme to create mood. It can take several forms: a very tightly synchronised musical commentary as used in the Walt Disney and Looney Tunes cartoons (the constant mimicing of action by music is actually known as 'mickey mousing'), a piece of mood music intended to enhance the emotional impact (as in the famous shower scene in *Psycho*) or a short piece to link one scene to the next (known as a 'bridge').

The composition briefs may include an underscoring assignment for a selected piece of video footage.

An extract from Goldsmith's hunt music for *Planet of the Apes* is included in the Edexcel *New Anthology of Music*, No. 44.

Different composers create effects in different ways. Some use timbre (the screeching strings in *Psycho*) others use rhythm (the nervous quavers in Jerry Goldsmith's hunt music for *Planet of the Apes*). Most commonly, though, it is the subtle use of harmony which sets the mood: minor keys for sadness, atonality and harsh discords for fear and tension, modulations to sharp keys for an uplift, imperfect or interrupted cadences to create anticipation.

If you submit music intended to underscore a scene be sure to show how the main musical features and sync points relate to the images. You could show these on a time line – an annotated graph which includes timings on a scale with short commentaries on the pictures and music where they appear.

In some cases film directors employ shock tactics and deliberately use music which is out of character. An example of this occurs in the film *Good Morning Vietnam* where the Vietnamese villages are bombed to the music of Louis Armstrong singing *What a Wonderful World*. However, if you intend to experiment with irony in this way there is always a danger that the examiner may fail fully to understand your intentions. Remember that it is the music that is being marked, not the concept.

Libraries

Libraries are pieces of 'wildtrack' music – in other words they are not intended to be an exact fit for the pictures. They usually consist of a suite of pieces to underscore most of the situations that might arise in a film and from which the director will pick extracts. A television documentary series like *World at War* (composer, Carl Davis) required various marches, laments and victory hymns as well as sea music for the navy and busy music for the factories and for battle scenes.

An example of a brief for a library is included in the sample questions: four extracts for a wildlife documentary set in Australia. The brief offers a choice of themes: outback, dingoes hunting, kangaroos, praying mantis, and sand storm.

You will need to think about timings for each of the extracts – on average about 45 seconds each. Variety is important. The extracts must include some static music as well as one or two short climaxes. Most important, they must be evocative. The outback music, for example, will have to depict the heat, the red sands and the emptiness: lots of bare intervals, harsh timbres (scraped cymbals are good here), perhaps a sampled didgeridoo (but avoid being too obvious). Try not to use too much melody as strong thematic material tends to distract from the spoken narration.

Jingles

Jingles may accompany a commercial or form the backing for a promotional film (sometimes known in the advertising industry as an 'informational'). The composer is usually commissioned to write a set piece around a series of film sequences although the end product will probably be fine-edited to fit the music.

The sample briefs include a score for a promotional video to launch a new four-wheel-drive vehicle: a three-minute soundtrack following a scenario in which the vehicle is seen driving across a beach in the spray, entering a cave from which it emerges in the Alps, then cutting to a montage of the seasons on a farm in the Yorkshire Dales and finally showing children being dropped off at school.

The secret of jingles is not to pack in too many ideas and to avoid changing the musical style too often. This jingle may involve, perhaps, only three main ideas; the beach, the Alps and the farm. There may be sync points within these sections (for example the spray on the beach picked out by 'splashes' in the music) but you should concentrate on finding a way of binding the whole thing together (a style or melody common to all or using the same instruments throughout).

This is a task where it will be essential to plan ahead by drawing up a time line and composing around it.

Cartoons It is rare to find a modern cartoon which requires an almost continuous underscore full of mickey-mouse techniques of the type heard in old *Tom and Jerry* cartoons. Note the sparing use of music in *South Park* and the *Wallace and Gromit* animated films, or the unobtrusive jazz-based improvisations which underscore the *Pink Panther* cartoons. Nevertheless cartoon music can give you ample scope to employ a variety of ideas, especially if you enjoy writing humorous music. They can thus make a good choice for an exam submission providing you avoid writing nothing more than a series of ten-second links that do not hold together well as a whole.

Computer-game music As a compositional task games music is not unrelated to cartoon music. It is generally on a smallish scale instrumentally: a MIDI ensemble, club-dance samples or a rock band – but electronic timbres are also suitable. One thing to remember is that because games are interactive and the outcomes depend on the players, games music rarely, if ever, builds to a climax in the way it so often does in a film. An exception is the type of game where there is an element of time running out, and where the games designer wants to instil a sense of tension. This is often achieved by a gradual increase in tempo or modulation through keys.

You would need to compose several sections to represent the levels of the game although it might be an idea to choose an existing game and provide a short description rather than spend time trying to invent one of your own – there are no marks for games design!

Songs

The composition briefs for the *Words and Music* area of study will usually include a brief for a song. You may be given the lyrics or there may be certain requirements regarding structure. For instance you may be told that the song has to include a chorus, a bridge or an instrumental solo.

As in all composition tasks the examiners will expect you to use technology. This could be achieved in any of the following ways:

✦ a song written for live performers, the recording of which has been produced by you

✦ a song which employs electronic or amplified instruments in its backing (this could include a computer-sequenced backing)

✦ a song which includes sampled material (possibly including sampled vocals)

✦ a score which has been produced and printed using scorewriting software.

Something which always seems to cause difficulties is how to record and/or notate the vocal part. It may be that you are not able to find a singer whom you think will be good enough for the recording but if this is the case bear in mind that the performance is not assessed. In cases where there are no singers available many candidates usually record the song with the vocal part played by an instrument, or provide a sequenced mock-up of the song using a sampled vocal timbre. If you have to resort to this it will be important to show how you have set the words and so you will need to provide the examiner with as much notated information as possible. A written-out (or printed) vocal part with underlaid words (such as a lead-sheet) is ideal, but such parts can be difficult to write out, especially if they are highly syncopated and you are not confident with rhythmic notation. You may find it helpful to get a bit of practice notating note values so you can tackle this task. In addition, study and play lead-sheets to gain a better understanding of how vocal music is notated. The *Busker's Books*, easily available in music shops will provide lots of material.

The example on page 69 shows how words need to be precisely underlaid below the correct notes.

Playing and analysing other composers' songs will be an important part of your preparation for any songwriting brief and you will find the work you do for the *Words and Music* area of study useful. In particular you should be familiar with the following:

✦ basic song structures and their components: blues, 32-bar song, turnaround, verse, chorus, middle-eight, bridge, introduction and coda

✦ how to establish a basic stylistic feel for the song in its backing: drum pattern, bass line, backing chords etc

✦ how to enhance the song with backing vocals, instrumental fills, orchestrations, solos and overlays (solo instruments playing along with the vocals).

Remember that singers need to breathe and the ear needs variety – make use of short instrumental licks in the gaps between vocal phrases and don't forget the importance of a memorable hook line that you can use in the choruses, intro and coda (or 'outro'). Adding a second vocalist later in the song can be particularly effective – either in dialogue with the main singer, or singing in harmony, or even just in octaves. Any of these can provide that vital variety.

Club dance

This is very popular with candidates although they tend frequently to underestimate how difficult it is to produce a good dance track – there is more to it than a couple of drum loops and a four-bar chord pattern. If you are interested in this music you will probably have your own preferences, be it decks, garage, drum and bass, and so on, but if you are intending to submit club dance for the exam it may be worth considering how some of the various styles relate to the mark scheme (see page 97) and how their various features might be developed, as the following examples show.

If you are unable to record your work with a strong vocalist you might consider compiling a vocal track from samples, but you would need to be quite skilled in the use of the sampler, especially the techniques of time-matching (stretching or transposing samples so they all run at the same bpm). If you intend to remix another song, it is important that you make it clear to the examiner what processes you have used and what your creative contribution was to the final result. You could include a recording of the original along with written documentation.

Garage

Trance Trance is often highly produced using lots of high-energy instrumental loops and striking timbres. Many songs are based on fairly traditional verse–chorus forms, and for the chorus you will have to master the knack of writing a chord sequence which, although in the minor key which is customary in trance, manages to sound bright rather than sad.

Drum and bass Drum and bass offers quite a lot of scope for special effects and synthesised timbres – especially ones that transform over time through modulation or filtering. There is a danger, however, that the piece might ramble and you will need to keep a tight control over the textures and repetitions in order to produce a coherent structure.

Techno Techno, like drum and bass, is primarily instrumental – which neatly avoids the problem of finding a singer! As with garage, though, the piece will tend to be determined by the level of your expertise with the sampler, since most techno is based on looped samples that often build into a very complex texture, combined with synthesised timbres. The trick is to avoid making it sound cluttered (which Prodigy, in particular, are very good at). Techno might be a good choice for a guitarist, as much of it is based on guitar samples.

Ambient Chill-out pieces are among the most popular of all for students, probably because textures based on dreamy string and synth pads are quite easy to organise on the computer sequencer. The difficulty is creating something original. Timbres for ambient pieces need to be interesting (try cross-fading or filtering several pads together) and the harmonies are usually doubled or chorused so they sound very rich. There is also quite a wide frequency range in the recorded mix (bright, sharp effects as well as the deep bass pulses you feel through your body). Although ambient tends to be rather static, formally the interest is maintained by the ways in which the individual loops shift and change in relation to one another, rather like a minimalist piece (see page 95).

Electroacoustic compositions

Electroacoustic music includes many different styles, but broadly it is art music that uses technology to create, explore and modify sounds in order to create new types of sonic experience. Pieces are often experimental, with a focus on timbre and space, rather than on using technology to mimic or enhance 'real' instruments.

The sample briefs in the *Words and Music* area of study include two pieces involving voices. One gives a choice of contexts, for example, 'people at prayer' and 'a foreign language'. The task is to compile recorded or sampled vocal materials relating to the chosen context and then arrange them as a musical collage.

Another sample brief involves a prose extract from a book (George Orwell's *1984*). The task here is to record performances of two settings of the words, one spoken and the other sung (you would have to compose both settings), and then edit these together to form a single coherent piece.

Collage is a popular electroacoustic technique, doubtless because it is relatively easy using sequencing or digital recording software. However you should heed the warnings in relation to sequenced compositions which appear throughout this chapter – it is all too easy to create a jumble of odds and ends which, although they might be interesting on their own, fail to add up to a whole. Always think about structure.

Many electroacoustic compositions involve the processing and transformation of timbres or samples and in these cases the slow unfolding of the sonic landscape *is* the structure. It takes great compositional discipline to sustain a slow-moving transformation; Stockhausen's *Hymnen*, though based on taped rather than sampled loops, is a slow meditation on national anthems from around the world, and Trevor Wishart's *Vox Cycle* includes a piece inspired by the Hindu god Shiva who transforms into a series of animals and insects.

These processes have inspired a generation of composers who prefer to work in the art gallery, rather than the concert hall, for which they compose sound installations. If you are thinking about submitting such a piece, be sure to provide adequate explanation about the way the sound relates to the physical surroundings.

Minimalism

Minimalism, music based on ostinati over static harmonies, has always been popular with music technology candidates, probably because the repetitions and textures are quite easy to manipulate using a sequencer. However minimalism is not normally thought of as a technology-based style. It is more commonly performed in a concert hall by live players, although the American composer Steve Reich used samples of New York street sounds (played live through a keyboard) in *City Life*.

The second movement of Reich's *New York Counterpoint* is a minimalist piece that uses a live clarinettist playing against ten backing tracks that the same player has recorded earlier. It can be found in the Edexcel *New Anthology of Music*, No. 12.

The main processes of minimalism could be summarised as follows, and, as you can see, all can be carried out quite easily with technology:

+ melody-based pieces – like Philip Glass' *Facades* which features a slow-moving instrumental lament accompanied by string chords in rather restless quavers

+ permutation pieces – in which an ostinato, or series of ostinati, is slowly transformed either melodically or rhythmically

+ phase pieces – in which an ostinato is played in **canon** and each part has a note or beat missing so the parts get out of time with each other but eventually come back together.

The recording

Whatever type of score you submit, remember that the recording will probably provide the best evidence of your ability to use technology creatively. The recording techniques which you have learned in the multitrack recording units should be applied here. The examiner will be looking for the same attention to detail and the same quality of presentation.

The score

There are various ways of notating compositions and you should choose one that is appropriate for the type of music you write. Scores can take various forms, including:

✦ A fully notated score. It is very rare in popular music to find all the parts given in full, although it is common in film scores or jingles where live players are involved in a recording session.

✦ A piano reduction (sometimes called a short score). This is a keyboard arrangement of the piece on two staves, sometimes with annotations to identify instruments or cues.

✦ A song sheet. This requires three staves for each line (system) of music. The top one is a vocal part with lyrics, the lower two contain an arrangement of the accompaniment for keyboard – this is the type of layout normally used for the sheet music you can purchase in music shops.

✦ A lead-sheet. This is a vocal part with lyrics below and chord symbols above.

Note that it can be quite tricky to create good vocal notation if you are unsure about the correct underlay of words. This may need practice (see the example on page 69).

✦ A chord chart. This is a common way of notating popular music, often found in so-called real books and fake books of songs and jazz standards. The basic structure of the song is provided on a blank stave with chord symbols above and any important riffs, bass lines, rhythms and voicings written in.

Not all music can be notated on conventional staves, though, and this includes club dance and electroacoustic compositions. For these you could try one of the following:

✦ A track diagram. Exactly like the track display on a computer sequencing program, this shows the instruments or samples and how they are organised in tracks.

✦ A flow chart. This is a diagrammatic scheme designed by the composer to show the main features of the piece, how one idea follows and relates to another, and what the component sounds and processes are.

✦ A graphic score. This can consist of artwork, grids or graphs to represent the key features of the piece. You can include written comments or footnotes. There is an example of an art-music score in this style in the Edexcel *New Anthology of Music*, No. 11 (notice how it uses extensive explanatory notes).

✦ A recording log. This may be helpful to show the technical processes involved in some types of studio-based composition.

What is important is that you make your intentions clear to the examiner and give enough detail for other musicians to recreate the piece with reasonable accuracy. Remember to identify the equipment used (including computer software) and to show the origin of any samples and material downloaded from the Internet.

Achieving a good mark

Compositions are likely to be assessed for:

+ quality of composition
+ effective use of technology
+ clarity of the score.

The quality of the performance of the piece is not assessed. This is one reason why it is important to provide as clear a score (or alternative form of documentation) as possible so the examiner knows what the composer intended in the composition even if it is not played very accurately.

Edexcel's published guidance proposes that marks will be awarded for compositions in the way outlined below.

Presentation

According to the feedback given by composition examiners more marks are lost for poor presentation than for any other criterion.

Marks are given for the score and the recording. The examiner will concentrate on the recording in the case of music which is not easy to notate, although any written documentation needs to be neat.

Marks in the top category go to work which shows attention to detail. Graphic scores and track diagrams should show how the ideas are organised, and give details of resources and important processes that were used. Scores (full scores or charts) should contain enough information for a reasonably capable group of session players to give a performance, and notated melodies and riffs should include all necessary dynamics and phrasing. Articulation marks should be included (these are particularly helpful to wind and string players). Recordings should show attention to balance, clarity, stereo image, dynamic and frequency ranges.

Marks in the middle range go to scores or documentation which are readable but lacking in detail (but more marks will be lost if important details like dynamics or tempo are missing). A recording may have some faults but not enough to detract from giving a sense of the composition.

Marks in the very bottom category go to untidy scores or documentation in which instrumental parts or important features are either missing or illegible and for recordings which are distorted or poorly balanced to the extent that the composition's main features cannot be heard properly.

Quality of outcome

This is a mark for the overall quality of the composition: how it engages the listener, how stylistically accurate it is and how well it fulfils the brief.

The highest marks go to ambitious pieces (which is not the same thing as *long*) where the student has clearly taken both the brief and the task of composing seriously. The style of the music will be well focused.

The lowest marks go to pieces which are short on ideas or duration (including excessive use of repeats to make up the length), which employ fewer than the four required parts/tracks or which are stylistically inconsistent or unfocused.

Use of resources Marks are given for the handling of the resources (instrumental as well as technological).

High marks go to work in which there are very few errors or misjudgements. Instruments and technology will have been used in a controlled and creative way with a secure understanding of their capabilities. In particular the work will show awareness of the differences between real instruments and their General MIDI counterparts. Writing for real instruments will be idiomatic and textures will be clear. Thought will have been given to the combination of electronic timbres.

Marks in the middle ranges are given to work in which instrumental parts are competently composed but dull in effect. Textures may be thin or continuous throughout much of the piece with little attempt at variety. There may be some errors of judgement or limitations in the use of technology but not enough to compromise the success of the composition.

Low marks are given to work in which instrumental parts are unsuitable for real instruments or which are unnecessarily difficult (or impossible) to play, perhaps because they go out of range. Technology will be used in a restricted way and there will be misjudgements which detract from the overall quality.

Coherence Coherence refers both to the overall structure of the piece and to its small-scale features, like harmony and melodic construction.

For a mark in the top range you need to produce a piece with a satisfying balance between repetition and contrast – although the examiners will be aware that some styles are by their nature more repetitive than others. Harmony will be well-judged and ambitious, with more complex chords (like 7ths or chromatic chords), contrast of key and possibly modulations between sections where appropriate to the style of the music.

Marks in the middle range will be given to work in which the structures are generally logical although there may be some misjudgements. Forms may be basic (simple ABA or strophic) but there will have been some attempt to articulate the form with varied material. Harmony will be controlled but probably unadventurous and confined to standard chord sequences.

Low marks are given to excessively repetitive work, or work which consists of a mere succession of unrelated ideas. There will be many uncomfortable moments in the harmony of such pieces as well as instances of carelessness such as wrong notes or misaligned parts.

Further reading

Useful guides to instrumentation are listed on page 67. In addition, the following book is full of ideas and techniques for composing in a wide range of styles, and it covers basic starting-points as well as more extended and advanced work: **The Composer's Handbook** by Bruce Cole. *Schott and Co Ltd*, 1996. ISBN: 0-946535-80-9.

Listening and Analysing (A2)

In the rest of this book we'll be looking at the kind of things you need to know to complete the listening test at the end of your A2 course. This consists of the two following equally-weighted parts.

Part 1: Controlling and interpreting MIDI data

You will sit this part of the exam at a computer equipped with sequencer software, a GM sound module, headphones, a music keyboard and a CD-player capable of playing audio files. Note that you will need to be able to read conventional staff notation for some parts of this test.

You will be given a CD-ROM disc containing an audio file of a piece of music and a MIDI file. There will be two sets of questions. In the first set you will have to identify differences between the score of the piece and the recorded version(s). You will also be asked to comment briefly on basic harmonic and melodic features of the music. This might include describing how a solo has been realised in performance, identifying keys and chords, and explaining chord symbols in the score.

For the second set of questions you will need to load the MIDI file from the CD into your sequencer and analyse the data in the file using the various editing screens available. The questions will ask you to comment on aspects of the data such as how the tracks are panned within the stereo field, how devices such as program change, aftertouch and pitch bend are used, how quantisation and tempo change have been employed, and how variety of articulation is evident in the precise note-lengths and velocity levels. There will also be questions on how musical interpretation could be improved by modifications to the data, and on topics such as how a bass drum part could be extracted from a drum-kit track, or how the rhythm of one part could be superimposed on the melody of another part.

You should be gaining experience in all of these aspects of MIDI in your own sequencing work, but we will look at some of the more technical issues in the next chapter.

You get ten minutes to set up and load the CD (which will work on PC and MAC systems only) and ten minutes to read through the questions. You then have one hour to complete Part 1. There will be a 30-minute break before Part 2 begins.

Part 2: Music technology in context

For this part of the exam you will have studied one of two topics: **either** *Music for the Moving Image* (see page 106) **or** *Words and Music* (see page 122).

Part 2 of the listening test takes one hour and consists of questions about the works you have studied, and their context. These are based on extracts of music recorded on a CD that you listen to on headphones. There will be sets of questions on both areas of study – you choose which to answer.

Helpful practice material for the listening tests is given in *AS/A2 Listening Tests for Music Technology* by Andy Collyer, Rhinegold Publishing Ltd, ISBN 1-904226-45-0. Workbook and Audio CD, each available separately. In addition, specimen and past papers are available from Edexcel.

Controlling and Interpreting MIDI Data

We took a brief look at MIDI on page 17, but we now need to explore this topic in the depth needed for the A2 exam.

MIDI files

Detailed information about MIDI files and how they are made up can be found at: http://ourworld.compuserve.com/homepages/mark_clay/midi.htm

MIDI was invented as a real-time link between different musical instruments, and so its messages are sent down a MIDI cable at the correct time. In contrast, a **MIDI file** (often known as a standard MIDI file, or SMF) is a way of storing a sequence of MIDI messages, either in computer memory or on a disk. It stores not only the messages, but also their relative order and the time at which they should be played back.

The basic structure of a MIDI file contains:

✦ tempo and time-signature information for the whole sequence
✦ MIDI messages, with details of when they are to be played.

Each of these elements is covered in the following sections.

Tempo track

There are two common types of MIDI file. In Type 0 files all the MIDI messages in the sequence are stored together in one track. In Type 1 files the MIDI messages for each instrument are stored in an individual track and there is an overall tempo track which applies to all instruments. Type 1 files are most commonly used with computer-based sequencers.

Every Type 1 MIDI file contains an overall timing track which stores information on the time-signature and tempo at the start of the piece, and whenever there is a change. You can usually view this information in your sequencer in a graphical or textual form. Find out early on how to do both of these on your particular sequencer. The example below shows how a segment of how such a tempo map might look in both graphical and textual forms.

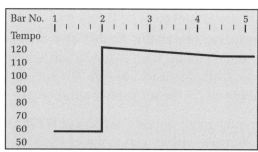

Bar/Beat	Event	Data
1:01:000	Tempo	60
2:01:000	Tempo	120
2:03:000	Tempo	119
3:01:000	Tempo	118
3:03:000	Tempo	117
4:01:000	Tempo	116
4:03:000	Tempo	115

Note that you could be asked to analyse a tempo track and explain how, for instance, a performance has been (or could be) made more expressive by slight fluctuations in the tempo.

This particular example shows a tempo of 60bpm at the start of the piece, followed by a doubling of speed at the start of bar 2, and an immediate rallentando. Note how the graph gives you a better idea of the overall flow of tempo, whereas the table shows more precisely what is happening at each point.

Types of MIDI message

MIDI information consists of messages for notes (on and off), pitch-bend, control, program change, aftertouch and system. All MIDI messages (apart from system ones) are associated with a particular MIDI channel. There are usually 16 available channels (although it is possible to have more if you have more than one **MIDI port**). Each channel is used to hold information about a specific instrumental part. For instance, you could set channel 1 to piano, channel 2 to violin, channel 3 to oboe, etc. Next we'll consider each main type of MIDI message in more detail.

MIDI has individual messages for note-on and note-off, but in a sequencer these are often combined into a single note event with a duration value (in beats, and beat fractions). Each note has its own **velocity** – a value between 0 and 127 which represents how fast the keyboard was pressed to generate the note. By now you should be absolutely clear that velocity (and not volume) is the main way to control the loudness of individual notes and thus obtain well-shaped, musical results. However velocity can also affect the timbre and attack of a note, depending on the characteristics of the sound being used.

The pitch of the note is also represented by a number in the range 0–127, where 60 is defined as middle C. 61 is therefore C♯, 62 is D and so on. On a sequencer you will often see notes referred to as C3 or F♯4, and you should learn where these are located on a keyboard with respect to middle C.

Pitch-bend messages represent what happens when a keyboard's pitch-wheel (or lever) is moved. All the notes on that MIDI channel are bent up or down in pitch. If you want individual notes (say, within the same chord) to have different amounts of pitch-bend they will need to be on separate MIDI channels. The range of the bend depends on how your sequencer shows it, but it is usually either 0–127 (0=fully down, 64=no bend, and 127=fully up) or at a higher resolution (from -8191 to +8192, with 0=no bend).

These messages allow a rich variety of control over the sound of an instrument and can help achieve an expressive MIDI performance. Different controllers are denoted by numbers in the range 0–127. Some of the most common (with their meanings) are:

0	Bank Select (see next page)
1	Modulation (vibrato)
5	Portamento time (portamento is a glide between notes)
7	(Part) Volume
10	(Stereo) Panning
64	Sustain pedal (on/off)
65	Portamento (on/off)
71	Timbre (usually 'resonance')
72	Release (adjusts the envelope release)
73	Attack (determines the envelope onset)
74	Brightness (affects the complexity of a sound)
91	Effect level (usually reverb level)
93	Chorus level.

Once you have established a controller's type you can interpret its value. It is a number in the range 0–127 and the meaning depends on the controller type. 'Type=7, value=127' means volume at full, while 'type=10, value=0' means pan fully left (where 64 is centrally panned, and 127 is panned fully right). In a sequenced piece you may see controllers used to set individual values (eg 'set reverb to full'). Alternatively you may see a whole stream of controller values to create a change over time. An example would be a series of decreasing volume controller values to create a fade-out (again, remember that volume is not the way to change dynamics – a diminuendo requires reduction of velocity, not volume).

Notes

In practice note-off is seldom used. Instead most devices use a MIDI 'running status' message to indicate that all further MIDI commands are of the same type until specifically changed. Notes are then switched off by sending a note-on message with zero velocity. This avoids having to transmit the type (or status) of every single event and the consequent reduction in data flow helps MIDI to respond more efficiently.

Pitch-bend

Controllers

A full list of MIDI controllers, with details, can be found at:
http://www.borg.com/~jglatt/tutr/ctl.htm

Aftertouch and system messages

Aftertouch and **system messages** can be implemented in different ways on different equipment. Aftertouch can affect volume, or timbre or something else – depending on your soundcard. System messages are often intended for specific pieces of MIDI equipment. You are unlikely to have to interpret system-specific data in a MIDI file set for the exam.

Program change

Program-change messages are used to assign a sound to a MIDI channel. A single program number is needed to specify the voice number required. You will usually encounter these at the start of the piece to select a groups of sounds – one for each channel. Sometimes you will see them in the middle of a piece to allocate a new instrument to a channel.

General MIDI

General MIDI also defines other parameters such as how drum sounds are to be assigned. For the full GM specification, and details of the more recent GM2 revision, go to: http://www.midi.org/about-midi/gm/gminfo.shtml For an overview (with sound examples) see: http://music.northwestern.edu/links/projects/midi/pages/genmidi.html

General MIDI (GM) specifies a set of 128 sounds (shown below) for synthesisers and sound cards so that when a MIDI file made on one GM system is replayed on different GM-compatible equipment it will seem reasonably similar. It won't be exactly the same, as only the names and numbers are defined – the actual sounds will vary slightly from one manufacturer to another. They include a range of useful instruments suitable for different types of music, and some sound effects. It is possible to have more than 128 sounds on a device by using **bank change** messages. These allow you to select one of many alternative 'banks' of 128 sounds, but these are not defined in the standard, and so will vary from machine to machine.

1 Acoustic Grand Piano	33 Acoustic Bass	65 Soprano Sax	97 FX 1 (rain)
2 Bright Acoustic Piano	34 Elec Bass (finger)	66 Alto Sax	98 FX 2 (soundtrack)
3 Electric Grand Piano	35 Elec Bass (picked)	67 Tenor Sax	99 FX 3 (crystal)
4 Honky-tonk Piano	36 Fretless Bass	68 Baritone Sax	100 FX 4 (atmosphere)
5 Electric Piano 1	37 Slap Bass 1	69 Oboe	101 FX 5 (brightness)
6 Electric Piano 2	38 Slap Bass 2	70 English Horn	102 FX 6 (goblins)
7 Harpsichord	39 Synth Bass 1	71 Bassoon	103 FX 7 (echoes)
8 Clavi	40 Synth Bass 2	72 Clarinet	104 FX 8 (sci-fi)
9 Celesta	41 Violin	73 Piccolo	105 Sitar
10 Glockenspiel	42 Viola	74 Flute	106 Banjo
11 Music Box	43 Cello	75 Recorder	107 Shamisen
12 Vibraphone	44 Contrabass	76 Pan Flute	108 Koto
13 Marimba	45 Tremolo Strings	77 Blown Bottle	109 Kalimba
14 Xylophone	46 Pizzicato Strings	78 Shakuhachi	110 Bagpipe
15 Tubular Bells	47 Orchestral Harp	79 Whistle	111 Fiddle
16 Dulcimer	48 Timpani	80 Ocarina	112 Shanai
17 Drawbar Organ	49 String Ensemble 1	81 Lead 1 (square)	113 Tinkle Bell
18 Percussive Organ	50 String Ensemble 2	82 Lead 2 (sawtooth)	114 Agogo
19 Rock Organ	51 SynthStrings 1	83 Lead 3 (calliope)	115 Steel Drums
20 Church Organ	52 SynthStrings 2	84 Lead 4 (chiff)	116 Woodblock
21 Reed Organ	53 Choir Aahs	85 Lead 5 (charang)	117 Taiko Drum
22 Accordion	54 Voice Oohs	86 Lead 6 (voice)	118 Melodic Tom
23 Harmonica	55 Synth Voice	87 Lead 7 (fifths)	119 Synth Drum
24 Tango Accordion	56 Orchestra Hit	88 Lead 8 (bass+lead)	120 Reverse Cymbal
25 Nylon string Guitar	57 Trumpet	89 Pad 1 (new age)	121 Guitar Fret Noise
26 Steel string Guitar	58 Trombone	90 Pad 2 (warm)	122 Breath Noise
27 Elec Guitar (jazz)	59 Tuba	91 Pad 3 (polysynth)	123 Seashore
28 Elec Guitar (clean)	60 Muted Trumpet	92 Pad 4 (choir)	124 Bird Tweet
29 Elec Guitar (muted)	61 French Horn	93 Pad 5 (bowed)	125 Telephone Ring
30 Overdriven Guitar	62 Brass Section	94 Pad 6 (metallic)	126 Helicopter
31 Distortion Guitar	63 SynthBrass 1	95 Pad 7 (halo)	127 Applause
32 Guitar harmonics	64 SynthBrass 2	96 Pad 8 (sweep)	128 Gunshot

Private study

1. What are the two basic elements of a MIDI file?

2. How would an accelerando be represented in a tempo track?

3. Which of the following is *not* a valid MIDI message: pitch-bend, sample-size, aftertouch, program change?

4. How many MIDI channels are available from a single MIDI port?

5. (i) What MIDI note number is given to the C above middle C?
6. (ii) Which note is represented by the MIDI note number 36?

7. How is a MIDI file different from a wav file?

8. What is the main advantage of using equipment that conforms to the General MIDI standard?

Viewing MIDI files in a sequencer

Sequencers usually have a main arrangement screen, which is divided into a number of tracks. It is normal for each track to contain MIDI data on a particular channel. When you load a MIDI file into the sequencer, each instrumental part should appear as a track on the main screen. You will need to select a particular track in order to display the information inside it. As described on pages 37–38, there are many editing screens that can be used to display MIDI information in different representations.

An event-list screen can be very useful for looking at all the MIDI information on a particular track in time order. For instance you will be able to see the program change message at the start of the track, which sets the instrument for that channel, along with maybe a volume controller and a reverb level. The event list is a good place to start when comparing the given score with the MIDI file. In the illustration *right* you will see a fragment of a musical score followed by a typical event list for the performance of this music.

Private study

In the list shown *right* the data for note events is in the form: note number, velocity, duration in beats (where beats are subdivided into 384 'ticks') and the data for controller events is type, value.

1. Identify the GM sound selected for this track, using the list on the previous page.

2. Why is there no tempo information in this event list?

3. What information appears in the list that is not in the score?

4. If the tempo was 60 beats per minute instead of 120, would the event list data look any different?

5. Where in the stereo field will this music sound?

6. What aspect of articulation has been ignored in the sequence?

7. Identify *three* different ways in which the note data could be changed to improve the musical expression so that it would sound more as if a human were playing it.

Bar/Beat	Event	Data
1:01:000	Prog. Change	12
1:01:000	Controller	91,127
1:01:000	Controller	7,64
1:01:000	Note	71,120,1:000
1:02:000	Note	73,120,0:192
1:02:192	Note	71,120,0:192
1:03:000	Note	76,120,1:000
1:04:000	Note	71,120,1:000
1:04:000	Note	75,120,1:000

As well as giving variety to the velocity levels in order to shape the articulation and phrasing of the music, you hopefully noticed in your answer to the last question that both the note-start positions and the note-lengths were far too regular, giving a very mechanical performance. Both of these features can be seen more easily on a grid edit (piano-roll) screen. This enables you to see the overall patterns of notes as well as subtleties of timing in the performance, such as which notes are played slightly before or after the beat.

The two examples below show how the music on the previous page might appear on a piano-roll display. The one on the left matches the sequence data we gave on the previous page and it should be obvious that it will sound very mechanical – the grid reveals the sort of regularity that can result from unedited step-time input. The example on the right shows a much more natural approach to rhythm and note-lengths. Far from being 'wrong', the position and length of the notes reveals the sort of variety that, combined with constantly changing and well-shaped velocity levels, can make a performance sound interesting and musical.

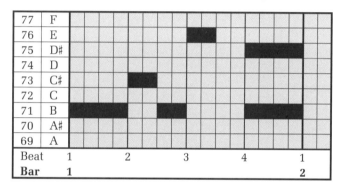 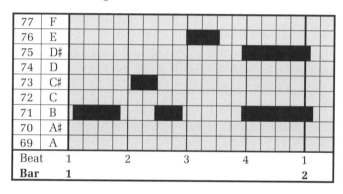

Note that it is not advisable to use a score editor to compare the sequence with the given score since the software has to make many approximations when converting numeric data into music notation and will often respond badly to timing subtleties – and score editors usually do not adequately represent controller information.

It is worth finding out how your sequencer represents controllers in a graphical manner. Some sequencers have a separate controller editor and others have a special viewing area immediately below the piano-roll screen. Take care that you select the correct controller number otherwise you may not see anything displayed. Pitch-bend and aftertouch are often viewed as if they were controllers, although in reality they are MIDI messages in their own right – they are not part of the 128 possible controller messages. Note that velocity can also be viewed in this manner and this is particularly useful for seeing how variation has been created in a musical line and how certain notes have been given special emphasis.

Analysing the data

The tiny example given above will give you some idea of what can be read and deduced from a MIDI file, but in the exam you will have to deal with many tracks and many more bars of music, as well as considering the tempo track.

Here are some more things to look out for when comparing a MIDI file to the score and acoustic recording of the music:

- Are there any major omissions? (eg no vocal line in the MIDI file because it is a backing-track)

- Is the MIDI version in the same key as the score and the audio recording?

- Are the musical parts the same (ie do the notes in the score correspond one-to-one with notes in the event list)? Remember that abbreviations in the score, such as a trill sign or tremolo, can result in many extra events in the MIDI file.

- Is there extra information in the MIDI file? (such as controller information altering the balance by changing the volume, or altering the pitch-bend).

- How does the use of panning in the MIDI file compare with the stereo placement in the recorded example?

Remember that you may be asked about how a particular musical phrase or event is constructed in the MIDI file. For example you might be asked to comment on how a guitar solo is realised, and the examiners will be looking for comments about which controllers are used (eg volume, modulation, pitch-bend) and how.

Finally it is likely that you will be asked to suggest how to improve the musicality/production of the file by editing the MIDI data. To do this listen carefully to the sound that the MIDI file makes when played through your soundcard. Concentrate on the section in question, and write down the limitations of what you hear. For instance there could be:

- excessive or uncontrolled pitch-bend
- inconsistent panning
- too much reverb or modulation
- inappropriate use of quantisation
- occasional notes in the wrong place
- no realistic gaps to suggest breathing in a wind part
- no variety in velocity levels in a particular part
- an inappropriate choice of GM sound
- 'dynamics' artificially created by fading a part in and out with the volume controller instead of using velocity
- poor shaping of tempo, such as no slight push of speed towards a climax or no relaxation at the end.

Then suggest the improvements you would make and explain how you would do this using MIDI messages.

Further reading

The MIDI specification is covered in detail in the book **Digital Sound Processing for Music and Multimedia** (see page 18) and its supporting website includes a chapter on MIDI:
http://www-users.york.ac.uk/~adh2/book/ch4.htm

An online MIDI tutorial can be found at:
http://www.borg.com/~jglatt/tutr/whatmidi.htm

Another good introduction to MIDI can be found at:
http://nuinfo.nwu.edu/musicschool/links/projects/midi/expmidiindex.html

Music for the Moving Image

Introduction

Remember that you should choose *either* 'Music for the Moving Image' *or* 'Words and Music' (see page 122) as your area of study.

This area of study (only applicable to A2) concerns the use of music in film and television. In particular it requires you to be familiar with two specific film scores, which will form the main focus of the exam. We will consider these later in the chapter but first let's look at the history and background of music in the movies, so that you have a context for your studies.

The development of music for film

Silent film has been viewed as a wonderful international art-form, not bounded by a specific language. You can read more about this at http://www.wastor.com/eng/film.htm

A useful summary of the history of film music can be found at:
http://www.americancomposers.org/hollywood_chihara_article.htm

The history of film music reaches back to the earliest cinematic experiments (by the Lumière brothers in 1895), when the sound of noisy projectors was masked by music played by a pianist or small band. As cinema gained popularity, and moved into the music hall, the resident pianist or pit orchestra learned how to enhance a film by setting a mood (eg romantic music for a love scene) and highlighting the action (eg a crash when someone fell over). Music for silent films reached great heights in movies such as *Birth of a Nation* (1915) where a large orchestra played, and guns and sound effects were sounded live behind the screen. Some cinemas built specially adapted pipe organs (fitted with extra percussion and more orchestral sounds) to accompany films.

Although we are focusing only on English-language films from the west, you should be aware that there are many other fascinating film-music cultures around the world. They developed after the introduction of sound-films, as movies became language-specific. For instance take a look at this site dedicated to *Filmi sangeet* – the Indian film song:
http://www.chandrakantha.com/articles/indian_music/filmi.html

The introduction of films with sound, specifically *The Jazz Singer* (1927) caused a revolution in the way music worked with film. Live performances dwindled, and composers were drafted in to provide recorded scores to accompany the film. Several well-established composers from the concert hall (such as Prokofiev, Copland, Walton and Korngold) found new audiences in the cinema-going public. However, film scores were to be gradually dominated by specialist composers writing purely for the movies. Max Steiner was the first of these and his evocative music for *King Kong* (1933) and Wagnerian-style score for *Gone with the Wind* (1938) established him as one of the great pioneers of film music.

Bernard Herrmann developed the art of film music, so that as well as accompanying the on-screen action, it gave psychological insights into the characters. *Citizen Kane* (1941) was the first of these, but he also wrote perhaps the most famous single piece of film scoring ever for the shower-scene in *Psycho* (1960).

Much detail about the background and plot of films such as *High Noon* can be found at: http://www.filmsite.org/

The popular-music industry met film music in the 1950s when the film *High Noon* (1952) shot to popularity following the advance release of the song *Do not forsake me oh my darlin'*. From that point on producers wanted marketable songs, and many composers felt that this grossly compromised their artistic integrity.

However, many great soundtracks were written involving popular music, not least John Barry's famous themes for the James Bond movies, and this trend has continued until today.

During the 1970s the orchestral soundtrack returned to popularity, primarily led by Steven Spielberg's collaboration with composer

John Williams. This began with *Jaws* (1975), and has continued until today with many films including *Close Encounters of the Third Kind* (1977), *Raiders of the Lost Ark* (1981), *E.T.* (1982), *Schindler's List* (1993), and *Jurassic Park* (1993). Williams also worked on George Lucas' *Star Wars* (1977) and all subsequent films in that series.

In recent years the Hollywood film market has been dominated not only by John Williams but by James Horner (composer of *Titanic*), Michael Kamen, Mark Isham, and James Newton Howard.

Sound synchronisation and reproduction

The development of the amplifier and loudspeaker had made the first sound films a practical proposition in 1927, but there were technical problems in keeping the soundtrack in synchronisation with the picture. Early attempts included pulleys linking projectors to gramophones. The most successful method was the optical soundtrack in which the sound is stored on the film itself, as a number of wiggly lines. These are read optically, fed to amplifiers, and thus to speakers.

The standard timing mechanism in film is called SMPTE code (see page 89). This code represents the number of frames (individual film images) that have elapsed from the start of the film. A similar mechanism exists for video. Those working with sequencers can (using the right equipment) synchronise the sequencer to the projector or video-player using MIDI Time Code (**MTC**).

The technology for the reproduction of sound in the cinema has been improving decade by decade. Not only have the acoustics of cinemas been studied, but the quality and number of loudspeakers has been steadily rising. Cinema-style surround sound has proved so successful that it has started appearing in home technology products such as televisions and computer-game consoles.

For an informative history of film sound see: http://history.acusd.edu/gen/recording/motionpicture.html

Function of music for moving images

Concert-hall music exists in its own right. It is an abstract art form, where listeners appreciate patterns of sound over time. Generally it doesn't set out to tell a story (except in the case of 'programme music' such as Tchaikovsky's *1812* overture). In contrast, music for film and television exists within the context of the pre-filmed images and thus the drama unfolding on-screen. In this respect its purpose is more like the music that has been used to accompany theatre since the time of the ancient Greeks.

The following article discusses the essence of music in the context of a film: http://www.filmsound.org/filmart/bordwell2.htm

Film music

Music cues in films are often relatively short, although longer passages are often needed for the opening titles, end titles and any scenes requiring musical illustration (battles, storms, love scenes and so on). Music can do far more than merely reflect the action, though. Motifs can be used to identify particular characters, scenes or events. These motifs can return in the underscore (the background music used throughout the film) to remind the audience of previous events or to hint at future events, without the picture or dialogue necessarily needing to refer to them explicitly. This technique can be traced back to Richard Wagner's use of the leitmotif in the 19th century. However, there is seldom the opportunity in films for the type of extended musical development of leitmotifs that Wagner employed in his operas.

Essentially the underscore acts as an unspoken language, and it is a language that can take many forms, including:

✦ illustrative music, such as Walton's thrilling depiction of the Battle of Agincourt in *Henry V*

✦ evocative music to suggest a place, such as the use of the Austrian zither in *The Third Man*, which is set in Vienna

✦ pastiche (music written in an old style) to evoke a bygone age or specific historical period, as in David Munrow's music for TV's *Six Wives of Henry VIII*

✦ dramatic music to enhance tension, as in the capture of the humans by the apes in Jerry Goldsmith's *Planet of the Apes*, or to ramp-up the effect of love scenes, as in Francis Lai's romantic score for *Love Story*

✦ comic music, sometimes using mickey-mousing in which on-screen events are faithfully followed in the score (eg sliding down a drainpipe might be accompanied by a descending xylophone scale and the dazed bump when the character hits the ground by a 'wah-wah-wah' from muted trumpets)

✦ music to enhance emotional impact, as in *Scott of the Antarctic* where the bleak score by Vaughan Williams accompanies the explorers' final doomed attempt to return to base, portraying in music the men's emotional states in a way that could not easily be expressed by pictures or dialogue in the film

✦ the use of leitmotifs to recall events, places and characters encountered previously in the film – sometimes developed into bridge passages that serve to link one scene with the next by underpinning the visual transition with musical continuity

✦ diegetic (or 'featured') music – that is music which is part of the action on screen, such as that heard when a character switches on the radio or walks past some buskers in the street

This last point should remind us that most film music is non-diegetic. It is something that is presumed not to be heard by the characters and is private to the members of the audience, enhancing their understanding and perception of events. Music forms a vital and intimate bond between the film and its audience, as well as serving the more mundane purpose of filling the silence that is a normal part of many film scenes.

Indeed, music can involve the audience in the plot in a more intimate way than even the characters themselves. Thus in *Psycho*, when the bank-worker Marion innocently takes a shower, Bernard Herrmann's spine-chilling score allows the audience to become aware of the danger to which she herself is totally oblivious, using music to anticipate the fatal stabbing of the knife through the shower curtain and thus heightening its impact (see page 120).

Television music

Although music for television inherits much from cinema music, it often has a different role to play. Lalo Schifrin (composer for the TV series *Mission Impossible*) describes how cinema audiences are captive and receptive, in a darkened room awaiting the slightest sound. In contrast he describes a TV theme (or signature) tune as having to 'shout out' to those in the kitchen, or talking in another room, that their programme is about to begin. Also the screen is smaller and thus the musical gestures need to be bigger. Admittedly much of this is changing with the introduction to the home of large-screen TV sets, and high-quality films on DVD with multi-channel sound.

The degree to which music is used on television varies considerably according to the type of programme. For instance soaps are mainly limited to title and diegetic music – the use of an underscore would sound very unnatural and remove the feeling of everyday life that is a key element. On the other hand, major wildlife documentaries may have almost continuous music on a very grand, film-like scale to enhance the natural spectacle (as in the recent BBC series *Blue Planet*), to avoid long silences because the interest is mainly visual, and also to signal their importance as prestigious, high-budget programmes that are intended to be taken seriously. Try keeping a TV diary for a week, noting how music is used in the programmes you watch.

Lalo Schifrin's home page can be found at: http://www.schifrin.com/

Music for advertising

Much of the music heard on television occurs in adverts. Here the jingle predominates – a short musical phrase, or sung catchphrase, which is intended to be memorable. Adverts also use a cut-down form of the cinematic mood language – especially when the mood changes in response to a product (eg sombre atonal music turning to happy, relaxed harmonious music when the headache tablet takes effect). Music may also be used to suggest a brand image – a grand orchestral or operatic excerpt to imply that a car has class, or cartoon-style music for sweets marketed at young children.

Music for computer games

Early computer games had notoriously 'bleepy' soundtracks that changed only for each level of the game. As computer games have become more sophisticated, and the technology to host them has become more powerful, their use of music has developed greatly. Much is borrowed from cinema in terms of setting the mood or catching the action. However a highly significant difference is that a film music composer works to a finished film (where all the timings are fixed), whereas the music in a game is determined in real-time by the actions of the player. This means that the composer does not know in advance how long each musical section should last, or when it will need to change into another section. Thus the act of composition for a computer game is potentially much more complex than for a film, since many musical elements need to be composed that can fit together in any order and repeat or transform for an unknown number of times.

Studying film music

For answers to many general questions on film music go to: http://www.webcom.com/~auricle/welcome-fmusfaq.html

This section considers some general questions which you can apply to any piece of music for the moving image. You should try to answer all these questions for each of the films you are studying. There are two sets of questions – the first on the whole film, the second on a particular musical extract (known as a 'cue').

Remember it is *essential* to view the films you study, and not just listen to their soundtracks. If you can find the time, give yourself permission to watch more films and television. Listen carefully and try answering these questions for different films.

Questions relating to the whole film

An excellent searchable resource for finding out about almost any film you can think of is the Internet Movie Database, at: http://uk.imdb.com/

Details of the music from films past and present (and interviews with composers) can be found at: http://www.soundtrack.net/

The magazine *Film Score Monthly* has its own searchable site at: http://www.filmscoremonthly.com/

✦ When was the film released?

✦ Who is the producer and what have they done before?

✦ Who is the composer and what films have they done before?

✦ What is the genre of the film (adventure, romance, horror, comedy, sci-fi etc) and what is the basic storyline?

✦ Is there a clear style to the music in the film?

✦ What instrumentation is used and is this consistent throughout the film? If not, how does it change?

✦ What is the basic purpose of the music in the film? (see the list of points on page 108).

When watching a film you may often become aware that the music is playing and yet you did not notice exactly where it began. This is a sign of a well-placed and well-written musical cue, so you will have to rewind, and listen carefully to how it came in. The following questions will help you to focus on how that musical cue works.

Questions for a specific musical cue

✦ When does the music enter?

✦ Why there in particular? What is happening dramatically at that point?

✦ How does it enter? Slowly, with thin, gentle textures? Does it fade-in? Is it a sudden entry? Does it synchronise with any on-screen action?

✦ What mood is the composer hoping you will feel? Do you?

✦ How is this achieved musically? What is happening in terms of harmony, melody, instrumentation and texture?

✦ What musical motifs are used? Have they been used earlier? If so, how are they developed here?

Further reading

A standard text is **On the Track: A Guide to Contemporary Film Scoring** by Fred Karlin and Rayburn Wright. *Schirmer* (1990). ISBN: 0-02-873310-X. Other books on film music can be found at: http://www.filmmusicstore.com/fmstore/bookabartand.html

Core Films

The core films for examination in 2006 and 2007 are:

✦ *Blade Runner* (1982) – music by Vangelis

✦ *E.T.* (1982) – music by John Williams

These two Core Films are set for examination in June 2006 and 2007. There are likely to be different Core Films in subsequent years.

Both are science fiction films that have achieved cult status – although they are very different, not only in their storylines but also in their musical scores. The music of *Blade Runner* is largely synthesised, with many sound effects, while that of *E.T.* is written for a large orchestra and is symphonic in style.

Different versions of both films have appeared on VHS and DVD, and various music excerpts have been released on CD. Some of these are listed below for reference, but remember that you do not need to know about the different versions of either film. Questions will focus on a given extract and you will be asked to comment on the music and identify the ways in which the composers have used musical techniques and devices to achieve their effects. Examiners will be looking for answers that use musical vocabulary accurately. For example, in answering the question 'How does John Williams suggest flying in the *Flying Theme*?' you should aim to include appropriate technical terms – 'the melody is based on rising 5ths and sequences, and is played by high strings accompanied by repeated horn chords', rather than 'it is high and fast'.

Edexcel advises that more recent, extended versions of the films may be used for study, but warns that questions will not be set on any scene that does not form part of the original version.

The notes below identify the melodic, harmonic and rhythmic devices in the cues but each score has its own special character. In the case of *Blade Runner*, where the music is mainly electronic, you should concentrate on learning the technology terms, while in the case of *E.T.* you should concentrate on being able to recognise the instruments of the orchestra and how they are used.

Blade Runner (1982)

The film of *Blade Runner* has appeared in two main versions. The 1982 original included (at the insistence of the studio) a happy ending and extensive voice-overs to help explain the plot. This was released on VHS by Warner Home Video (PES 70008). In 1992 the 'Director's Cut' of *Blade Runner* appeared, in which the voice-overs were removed and the ending was made much more ambiguous, as originally intended. This is the version you will get if you buy a current retail DVD of the film (and is the one included in the very expensive 'Limited Edition Collector's Set' of *Blade Runner*).

Availability

The video of the original version forms a good basis for study. Although no longer available new, copies can often be found on ebay and from other second-hand sources, as well as in video rental stores.

There are at least two different versions of the music from *Blade Runner* available on CD. The first, originally released on cassette in 1982, is an orchestral adaptation by the New American Orchestra of eight musical highlights from the film. It is so unlike the original soundtrack that it should *not* be used for exam study.

In 1994 Vangelis released a CD of 12 tracks based on *Blade Runner* (East West Records, 4509-96574-2). Although sometimes described as the 'original soundtrack', this CD includes some new music and occasional reworking of the original film tracks. It doesn't include all of the music from the film and the tracks that are included don't always follow the same order as those in the movie.

Although this CD differs from the film in some respects, the sound quality is much better than that of the original film.

The composer

Vangelis (pronounced 'Van-gay-liss') is the name adopted by the Greek musician, Evangelos Odysseas Papathanassiou (born 1943). He was a pioneer of popular electronic music and the 'New Age' style, and released a series of studio-based albums from the 1970s onwards. Vangelis has also written a number of film scores – his theme music for *Chariots of Fire* (1981) has become something of an anthem, played at moments of sports drama, especially on the athletics field. He composed the FIFA world cup song in 2002 but declined an approach from the progressive rock band *Yes* as a possible replacement for keyboardist Rick Wakeman.

For more on Vangelis see www.elsew.com/ and look out for the creation of the planned website at www.vangelisworld.com

The film

Blade Runner was directed by Ridley Scott, whose other films include *Alien* and *Gladiator*. It is set in Los Angeles in 2019, which must have seemed a long way off in 1982 – there is an apocalyptic darkness about the images (the multi-layered sets and photography are spectacular) which still makes it feel futuristic today. Ray Batty (played by Rutger Hauer) leads a group of androids, called replicants, with a built-in life expectancy of four years who mount an attempt to force their manufacturers to extend their life span. Rick Deckard (played by Harrison Ford) is the cop who tracks them down. *Blade Runner* was one of the first films in the cyber-punk genre, and while it is primarily an action film many commentators have suggested sub-plots and allegories involving life, death and immortality, slavery and revolution, good and evil.

For more on the film, see www.brmovie.com/

The score

The score for *Blade Runner* was composed when digital technology was still in its infancy. The electronic timbres have a rich, analogue quality in contrast to the brighter and harder digital sounds we are more accustomed to today. The music, which was nominated for a BAFTA award in 1983, includes some memorable saxophone work by Dick Morrisey and vocals by Mary Hopkin and Demis Roussos, both of whom had enjoyed successful recording careers during the 1970s. Hopkin was a discovery by the Beatles, promoted as a folk singer and signed to their Apple label; Roussos, a fellow Greek countryman and long- term collaborator of Vangelis, was a gold-selling middle-of-the-road balladeer.

The following notes are based on the 12 cues featured on the CD soundtrack recording from East West Records, with additional notes to explain some of the differences between these tracks and the cues in the original 1982 film. Unfortunately, in the latter much of the musical detail is obscured by dialogue, sound effects and foley (the technical term for sound effects such as traffic noise, the hum of air conditioning or the rustle of clothing).

1. Main Titles

The film opens with distant electronic explosions and a simple fanfare (of the type made famous in *Chariots of Fire*) played by an unaccompanied sine wave (neither of which are included on the CD). There are many sound effects and clips of dialogue mixed in with this CD track (and on some of the other tracks also), and it is at times difficult to distinguish between these and the effects added by the composer, such as white noise (which sounds like rushing wind) and siren-like instrumental glissandi.

This opening track is built over a sustained string chord. Note the intervals which the composer adds over the prevailing drone –

minor 3rds and augmented 4ths – which underline the gloomy, menacing nature of the scenery. Against this background come short, sparkling arpeggios played on the celesta (always a good way to enhance a air of mystery) and slow-moving string glissandi. Notice also how the music moves into the major from the implied minor of the opening as the action commences.

2. Rachel and Decker Meet

Sustained sounds also dominate this cue. Here Vangelis has created a counterpoint of layered wave forms to underscore the dialogue (which is included on the CD) and you can hear clearly the smooth sine waves contrasting with the harsher square waves. On the CD this texture develops into a simple minimalist-like ostinato over a one-bar drum pattern with subdivided beats (not unlike the backing loops of some of Björk's songs) although this part of the cue is not audible on the film soundtrack.

In the action which follows there are a number of references to music that will be heard later. As Decker begins his search for the replicants we hear a fragment of track 9 from the CD and during the subsequent long scene between him and Rachel, when the love interest begins to develop, we hear the music of track 8. The first appearance of Pris, Batty's female replicant partner, is accompanied by 'Blade Runner Blues' (track 7). Decker searching the market for the nightclub-dancer replicant is underscored by a cue not included on the CD but related to track 10. Here there is a more pronounced eastern influence, with modes involving the melodic interval of an augmented 2nd and a tabla backing with the beat subdivided middle-eastern style into 3+3+2.

3. Wait for Me

This is not heard on the film soundtrack. As in the track 2 there is some dialogue mixed in with this cue, which consists mainly of a hypnotic backing made up from repeating two- and four-chord sequences with a simple saxophone melody above.

4. Rachel's Song

This, too, is not from the original film. A pattern of xylophone and other synthesised mallet timbres (like dripping water) forms the backing for a wordless solo from Mary Hopkin. Her folk-like voice with heavy reverberation, along with the dorian mode, creates a strongly Celtic feel, similar to the score composed by the Irish band Clannad for *The Last of the Mohicans* (1993), and which featured Enya on vocals. The cue ends with the melody repeated by synthesised violin, another sine-wave-generated timbre.

A song without words is sometimes called a vocalise (pronounced *vocal-ease*).

5. Love Theme

We first hear this music when Deckard in his flat looks through albums of photographs of Rachel. He is clearly attracted to her but afraid she is a replicant. The cue consists of a saxophone solo supported by lush string chords and is in ternary form. The electric piano solo in the middle section sounds like a Fender Rhodes – a popular instrument at the time. Later, when Rachel and Deckard are alone together, she plays the piano over this cue and it develops into the only one where the music closely follows the action. As they argue briefly and she goes to leave (before finally kissing him) the music becomes increasingly dissonant, stressing the flattened 6th degree of the scale, which imparts a very wistful feel to the music, before relaxing once again into the lazier saxophone melody.

6. One More Kiss, Dear

Diegetic is explained on page 108.

This song is heard after Deckard has killed the nightclub-dancer replicant and is café music heard in the street (in other words it is diegetic music). It is a pastiche song in 1930s' style, with a backing combo of piano, upright bass and drums (played with brushes). The vocal emulates the style of the 1930s' singer, Al Bowlly, famed for singing through a megaphone. The 32-bar structure of the song is absolutely in style, down to the spoken part in the middle eight and the call-response dialogue between voice and trombone. (Not all of this musical detail is audible in the film.)

7. Blade Runner Blues

This cue is heard several times in the film, including during the chase and during the shooting mentioned above. It is a long cue, and is not strictly a blues, although the melody does feature a 'blue' flattened 5th. Analogue sounds are particularly obvious in this cue – rich string chords and the square-wave lead synth solo.

8. Memories of Green

A solo for detuned piano in romantic ballad style and with many effects – reverberation, background glissandi, bleeps, short-wave radio interference and sirens. Vangelis adapted it from a track of the same name on his 1980 album *See You Later*, which featured a background of sounds from an early computer game.

9. Tales of the Future

This cue appears several times in the earlier part of the film – in the snake-charmer scenes at the nightclub and at the start of the final confrontation between Batty and Deckard. However, it is not heard in full during the film.

The track features Demis Roussos, his trademark falsetto here sounding like an unearthly call to prayer. The lyrics resemble Arabic words but are actually mainly gibberish. The eastern influence is supported by sitar-like strings, gongs, Indian cymbals, LFO (low frequency oscillation) drones and a saw-tooth sound from the lead synth that resembles an Indian double-reed instrument called a shenai. Many of the pitches are shifted a quarter-tone, giving the music a raga-like feel. This cue segues with the next.

Segue (pronounced 'seg-way') is an Italian word meaning 'follows'. In music it is used to indicate that the next item should follow without a break.

10. Damask Rose

The Asian influence continues with a string solo. Here the raga-like basis of the melody is more evident than in the previous cue. It ends, like many others in the film, with electronic wind sounds and windchimes.

The climax of the film, the hunt and chase between Deckard and Batty, opens with fragments of tracks 1 and 9. We also hear a new cue, not included on the CD – celesta chords descending creepily in semitones. Much of the soundtrack for the chase is provided by Batty himself, who emits eerie vocal sounds and hoots to frighten Deckard in the darkness. Batty dies before he can kill Deckard, his final speech being underscored by track 12. In the final scene Deckard goes to find Rachel and, with a reprise of track 5, kisses her and she wakes up (rather like a prince and the sleeping beauty).

11. Blade Runner (end titles)

This is the only CD track to appear in its entirety and is the only up-tempo cue in the film. The backing is an ostinato in the bass, which shifts up and down an urgent minor 3rd, with an insistent snare-drum pattern. Note the other percussion: interjected tubular bells, timpani and brass chords.

A slow-moving celesta melody like a fanfare, punctuated by bass-drum effects. In the film this track accompanies a scene in which the last of the runaway replicants is about to be terminated.

E.T. (1982)

E.T. – The Extra-Terrestrial is another film that exists in two versions – the original 1982 movie (which received a PG certificate) and the version made for the restoration and re-release of the film in 2002 (the 'anniversary edition'). The latter omits several shots (such as the guns carried by the police chasing E.T. in the final scenes) in order to secure a U certificate, but adds in some material that had not been used in 1982. The many technical improvements include enhanced visual effects and a remastered soundtrack.

Both versions have been released by Universal in various formats, including wide-screen and standard DVD – those labelled 'Special Edition' are of the 2002 film. Look out for a second-hand copy of the two-disc 'Limited Collector's Edition' or three-disc 'Ultimate Gift Boxed Set' as they both include the original 1982 film, as well as the 2002 edition. The VHS video of the original movie can also still be found on sale from second-hand sources such as eBay.

The first album of music from *E.T.* was issued in 1982 on vinyl and cassette (later transferred to CD), and consisted of eight movements intended as a concert suite. Although based on the film score, these eight tracks don't match the soundtrack in detail. In 1996 MCA at last released a CD of 18 cues taken from the soundtrack (MCAD-11494), and followed this with a CD of 21 cues taken from the soundtrack of the 2002 'anniversary edition' (MCA 112 819-2). At the time of writing, both CDs of the soundtrack have been deleted in the UK, but you may well be able to find the 2002 'anniversary edition' (in particular) for sale second-hand or as an import.

The version of the 'Flying Theme' from *E.T.* in the *Edexcel New Anthology of Music* (NAM 45) is taken from this concert version and is therefore not identical to the music heard on the film soundtrack. Analytical notes on NAM 45 can be found in the *Rhinegold Student's Guides for Edexcel AS and A2 Music*.

The notes that follow are based on the original film although there are references to the 2002 'anniversary edition' and the anniversary CD. There are a number of (mainly small) differences between the versions, the principal one being that the 2002 film is slightly longer because it includes more scenes in the early stages of the plot, when Elliott and E.T. are getting to know one another.

Here are the 21 cues on the 2002 'anniversary edition' CD. Not all are present in the 1982 film, and some are run together to form a single cue, but the list provides a broad guide to the major scenes (tracks 1, 3 and 4 are not found on the 1996 CD):

1. Main titles
2. Far from home / E.T. alone
3. Bait for E.T.
4. Meeting E.T.
5. E.T.'s new home
6. The beginning of a friendship
7. Toys
8. 'I'm keeping him'
9. E.T.'s powers
10. E.T. and Elliott get drunk
11. Frogs
12. At home
13. The magic of Halloween
14. Sending the signal
15. Searching for E.T.
16. Invading Elliott's house
17. E.T. is dying
18. Losing E.T.
19. E.T. is alive!
20. Escape / Chase / Saying goodbye
21. End credits

The film

For more about the film see
www.etfansite.com/

E.T., directed by Steven Spielberg and with music by John Williams, is one of the most successful children's adventure films of all time, ranking alongside *The Wizard of Oz*. It won four Oscars, including one for its music, and tells the story of a family of children who befriend a stranded alien and help it return home. The film is remarkable for the way in which it ignores the long-established Hollywood tradition of depicting aliens as scary invaders in favour of portraying E.T. as lovable and vulnerable.

There are many echoes of other children's stories, particularly *Peter Pan* (a secret, magical visitor that only the children can see), and it has been suggested that E.T.'s luminous 'magic finger' was an idea taken from Michelangelo's illustrations in the Sistine Chapel. Other commentators have pointed to the 'death and resurrection' element of the story and to the setting in a modern context – the children are from a single-parent family, rather than a well-to-do one as in *Peter Pan*. The film is also memorable for its groundbreaking technology in the animation of the character E.T., and much of the camera work was shot at low level to suggest a child's point of view, particularly in scenes involving menacing adults.

The composer

Sony maintain a webpage on John Williams at www.johnwilliamscomposer.com/ – but it is limited to a few not very current news stories. The following website, although not always complete or well organised, may be more useful: www.johnwilliams.org/

See pages 107–8 for more about leitmotifs.

John Williams (born 1932) is perhaps the most successful composer in cinema history. Of the ten best-selling films, Williams wrote the music for seven – and his score for *E.T.* won, in addition to an Oscar, a BAFTA, a Golden Globe and a Grammy. Much of the popular appeal of Williams' music comes from his willingness to revive traditional approaches that others might regard as old-fashioned. These include bold, sweeping themes based on diatonic melodies and simple triadic harmonies, and a preference for the colourful textures of a full orchestra (although he often deputes the work of orchestration to others) rather than those of a small ensemble, jazz or rock group, or the sounds of electronically-generated music. Also important is his use of memorable leitmotifs that can be readily associated with particular characters and elements of the plot. Leitmotifs are particularly evident in Williams' score for *Star Wars*, although the technique is also to be found in *E.T.*

The score

John Williams bases much of the music in *E.T.* around the motif of a rising perfect 5th, which forms the basis of the famous 'Flying Theme' as well as many of the other melodic ideas. The rising 5th (often felt to have a rather heroic sound) is a favourite melodic interval of Williams, and appears prominently in many of his most famous tunes, such as the title theme to *Star Wars* (see *left*).

The character of E.T. is represented by the 'Flying Theme' and by a variation of it based on the mixolydian mode (see *left*). The latter has a somewhat wistful feel and is often saved for moments of sentiment or sadness. A derivative of this, usually in running quavers (C, B, C, G, F♯, E, D) appears at moments of urgency, such as when Elliott's brother Michael is searching for the missing E.T. The officials searching for E.T. are heralded by a motif (called 'the Government Theme' by some writers) which again starts with the unifying rising 5th (C, G, E♭, B). This is usually played by the horns and trombones and is preceded by a solemn repeated note. Yet another transformation of the 'Flying Theme' (the start of 'Far from home') is also shown *left*.

The main titles consist of sound effects – electronic drones and voices – over which is heard a fragment of the 'Flying Theme' played on a solo flute. This is followed by a statement of the 'Government Theme' and a hymn-like melody, harmonised in block chords, that is later used in E.T.'s dying scene.

The next few scenes, during which Elliott searches his garden and shed (convinced that something is hiding there) and finally comes face to face with E.T., are treated slightly differently in the two versions of the film. However, the music follows essentially the same pattern, starting with a repeat of the sound effects from the main titles and underscoring the early meeting with dissonant harmonies to maintain a sense of unease and mystery (the 'Alien Theme'). Only when Elliott puts down bait to lure E.T., does the music change from dissonant to consonant – a gentle dance-like melody scored for harp dispels the unease and signifies that E.T. is harmless. This cue is repeated later in the film when E.T. heals Elliott's cut finger.

The scenes depicting Elliott getting to know the Extra-Terrestrial involve an interesting set of cues because the action cross-cuts between the innocence of the children playing with E.T. and the menace of the officials searching outside the house. When Elliott first talks to E.T., the speech is underscored by a simple, clarinet melody which is reprised very tellingly later in the film when E.T. comes back to life. During these scenes the music switches between different versions of the rising-5th motif including the 'Government Theme' and a short burst of the 'Flying Theme' when E.T. magically revives a dead flower.

The next major scene also involves cross-cutting, this time between Elliott at school in a biology lesson and E.T. alone at home, exploring the house and finally getting drunk on beer from the fridge. The music follows the action very closely, starting with tense, sustained notes in the strings, a dance-like ostinato for the drunken action and for the chaos when Elliott releases the frogs in the biology classroom, and a burst of romantic melody (like the title theme of *Gone with the Wind*) when he kisses one of the girls.

The Halloween party features the film's famous 'flying sequence' and is preceded by an attractive neoclassical dance for woodwind as the characters parade in fancy dress. A series of modulations leads to the 'Flying Theme' itself – the well-known soaring violin melody with its upward-climbing melodic sequences. This also includes another device favoured by John Williams – the tonic chord followed by a major chord on the supertonic over an unchanging tonic bass (C, D/C).

The scene in which E.T. and Elliott use a home-made transmitter to send a signal to E.T.'s planet begins a sequence of events that leads the film's climax. The accompanying music is based on a development of the rising 5th theme. In the next cue this develops into the running-quaver version of the motif as Michael searches on his bicycle for the missing E.T, whom he eventually finds, ill and exhausted, by a river. The seriousness of the situation is underlined by a return of the funereal hymn-like melody, first heard in the titles.

The last cues together form a tightly-knit symphonic structure as the story takes us through a kaleidoscope of emotions; from the terror of E.T.'s capture, through death, rebirth and the final chase with Elliott to the space ship for the goodbye and escape.

The approach of the government officials to the family home opens with seven loud strokes on the timpani. Over a tense, sustained string chord E.T. is taken with Elliott to a medical facility outside the house. As Elliott pleads with E.T. not to die we hear the 'Flying Theme' in the minor key with the 5th motif descending in sequences as death approaches. A simple violin melody underscores E.T.'s death, followed by a telling reprise of the clarinet melody, first heard when ET and Elliott met. Then, Elliott notices that E.T.'s flower (a recurring image in the film) has come back to life and the 'Flying Theme' returns, now in a major key.

Elliott and E.T.'s escape is underscored by pounding ostinati, rising sequentially in pitch, with urgent fanfare-like outbursts. Williams' score follows the action with one motif after another as the action cuts between the children escaping on bicycles and the pursuing officials in their cars and, as the bicycles take to the air, we hear the 'Flying Theme' again.

The goodbyes are made over a long build up, modulating quite rapidly and never settling on a key until the end. when the 'Flying Theme' accompanies the take-off of the space ship. A simple coda, based on the mixolydian version of the motif, creates a sad ending, after which the 'End Credits' open with some of the main themes played by a solo piano, forming a textural relief after the thick orchestration of the film's climax.

Related film scores

Although the assessment will focus on the two works outlined above in the summer 2006 and 2007 exams, Edexcel recommends that you extend your studies to include related films. This should include a familiarity with other scores by the core composers as well as other films in the same genre.

The original musical soundtracks for the *Star Wars* trilogy are available on double CDs from RCA: 09026 68772/3/4.

No study of the science fiction genre would be complete without reference to John Williams' scores for the *Star Wars* trilogy, which include a wide range of musical styles and techniques. The main theme, whose opening phrase forms Luke Skywalker's motif (see the example on page 116), is a typical Williams melody. It rises triumphantly, based on perfect intervals, giving it a fanfare-like quality (a feature also found in *Raiders of the Lost Ark*, *E.T.* and *Jurassic Park*). The march-like theme of *Star Wars* recalls many of the title themes of World War II films like *Battle of Britain* and *Reach for the Sky* which, like *Star Wars*, celebrate the heroic daring of fighter pilots.

Jerry Goldsmith's score for *Planet of the Apes* (1968 version), which was discussed in the previous edition of this guide, also makes a good subject for study. Compare it with that other science fiction cult classic from the late 1960s, *2001: A Space Odyssey*, in which the soundtrack consists of a range of featured orchestral excerpts from concert-hall repertoire.

Other film genres

Edexcel recommends study of three genres from the following list: science fiction, thrillers, horror films, comedies, soaps, sitcoms, romantic films, westerns, wildlife films and documentaries. None of the core composers has a strong association with the western, and so Ennio Morricone's scores for the 'Fistful of Dollars' films, the most famous of which is *The Good, the Bad and the Ugly* (1966), should be regarded as essential listening. These, and many other films in this genre at the time, were known as 'spaghetti westerns' because they were financed and directed by Italians. They were usually filmed in Europe (often Spain) rather than the USA.

One of the most famous scores in the genre of horror movies is that composed by Bernard Herrmann for the film *Psycho*. When the film was released in 1960 it caused a sensation and broke new ground in its use of suspense. Although on video today it only rates a 15 certificate, the opening sequence, in which the main character Marion Crane and her lover are seen together in a hotel bedroom, was considered very explicit by the American standards of the time. However, it was the suspense scenes, and the killing of the main character less than halfway through (in the famous shower scene with its unforgettable music), that made *Psycho* a classic.

The director, Alfred Hitchcock, chose to shoot the film in black and white and this prompted the composer to write a score for string orchestra – a monochrome instrumental texture for a monochrome film. The rightness of this decision is apparent from the very opening where the title sequence (shot in black and white with no grey) is accompanied by a string texture in which there is a similar contrast of extremes.

Short, semitonal melodic figures and chordal stabs are repeated at great speed, transposed up and down, block-like, between the instruments – a musical equivalent of the black-and-white lines which sweep across the screen wiping each set of credits. A more lyrical melody tries to establish itself but is interrupted each time by the nervous rhythm of the stabbing chords. These interruptions give the opening music a very dislocated, anxious feel.

At the start of the action there is an example of a bridge (a musical link which finishes off the last sequence and prepares the viewer for the next). Herrmann halts the twittering energy of the title music and, as the camera pans across the city of Phoenix, Arizona for the start of the story he relaxes the viewer with sustained, descending chords. These are based on Am^6 and the added 6th imparts a static, drifting quality to the harmony. This chordal bridge is repeated many times in the film when Herrmann wishes to relax the tension – although, by the end, when we are feeling rather more jumpy, he is able to use it to achieve the opposite effect.

Soon after, we hear another idea which Herrmann uses extensively when he wishes to build tension. This is first introduced in the scene when we realise that Marion has decided to steal some money. Hitchcock introduces this suspicion in the viewer's mind with great subtlety, and music plays a key role. First we see Marion packing. Then the camera slowly pans across the bed where the envelope

A *Student's Guide to GCSE Music for the AQA Specification*, published by Rhinegold Publishing, includes a helpful chapter on several different genres of film music.

Bernard Herrmann: *Psycho*

The music for the shower scene has been included on a number of CD compilations and the film is available on video: *The Hitchcock Collection*, Universal: 061 0433.

of money is resting. The camera lingers for a moment, then an insistent three-note motif starts. This is repeated sequentially a tone lower, then played again at the original pitch. The music acts almost as a thought bubble. Note that, as in the title music, Herrmann relies upon repetition of a phrase transposed up and down – a device copied by many later film composers.

Perhaps the most memorable music in *Psycho*, however, is the cue for the shower scene. This scene lasts only 45 seconds, but took seven days to film, and famously shows not a single close-up detail of the violence. The horror is based partly on visual suggestion but principally on the sound of the knife going into the body and of the music. Starting with violins the strings play repeated, high, fast, ascending glissandi. It has been observed by countless analysts of this music that the pitch and timbre almost exactly replicate a human scream. The other instruments take this up. As the body falls to the floor Herrmann, as in most of his cues, relies on a change of timbre and register. The shrill violin glissandi are replaced by the cellos and basses playing an ostinato which features strong alternate up-and-down bow strokes like deep, panting breaths.

Hitchcock and Herrmann chose to avoid a strong musical ending. The final credits consist of a simple chromatic phrase which is taken up canonically by the instruments, building into a slow-moving and dissonant (but quite spooky) counterpoint.

James Horner: *Titanic*

The music soundtrack of *Titanic* is available on CD (Sony Classsical SK 63213) and the video is available on Twentieth Century Fox 0421S.

The Oscar-winning *Titanic* (1997) is a film in a very different genre. From the start it was conceived as a blockbuster, trading on public fascination for the great ship and its tragic sinking in 1912. The composer, James Horner, succeeded in capturing some of the class divide between the fictional main characters and their social backgrounds: Rose (wealthy, English upper class) and Jack (poor, Irish immigrant). This is partly illustrated in the diegetic music which can be heard throughout the film – sedate ensembles scored for chamber groups of strings and woodwind for the first class saloons and traditional Irish reels for the ceilidhs below decks in steerage.

The opening titles consist of original film footage of the ship leaving port, and the music is based on traditional Irish melody played on a tin whistle (Horner has long been interested in Celtic musical traditions). This is Jack's music and it is progressively developed to follow his character throughout the movie. It is usually unac-companied so that its appearances are carefully understated and its mournful quality serves constantly to remind the audience of the tragic nature of the story. It eventually forms the introduction to the hit song, *My Heart Will Go On*, heard during the final credits.

Not until the ship sets sail and heads for the open sea does Horner use the full orchestra. He also uses a wordless choir, which is supplemented by synthesised voices. In a 1997 radio interview, Horner said of *Titanic*: 'I was very nervous about using a big orchestra because I didn't want it to be some big Hollywood 1940s sinking spectacle. I was looking for something really very personal and human, which is why I chose the voice. And I used the synths to give it a slightly contemporary feeling and also a slightly timeless feeling at the same time.'

This first large-scale orchestral cue is published in the *Edexcel New Anthology of Music* (No. 47) and demonstrates Horner's clever use of harmony and interval. The opening modal fragment includes an augmented 4th in a five-note scale (see *right*). The word-less choir which sings it suggests, perhaps, sirens or mermaids (a possible borrowing from Debussy's *Nocturnes*) and the raised 4th degree (A♮) creates a sense of expectation and uplift. This sense is developed further as the music modulates rapidly from E♭ through G major and B major – up a major 3rd each time – as it moves through increasingly sharp keys to create a bright and optimistic mood.

augmented 4th

The cue also serves to introduce two of the film's main themes. One is based on Jack's Irish melody, performed by the choir and featuring many rising intervals to create a sense of hope. The other, which might be thought of as Rose's theme, is also derived from folk music. It is strikingly similar to the expansive orchestral melodies of Vaughan Williams, which are often related to folk music, with their march-like metre and characteristic use of the mixolydian mode (the major scale with flattened leading note) giving them an unmistakably stately and 'British' feel.

The music of the climax of the film – the sinking – is handled interestingly. Most of the initial scenes are accompanied by the ship's band which, true to eyewitness reports of survivors, plays on deck in an attempt to keep the passengers calm. As the ship starts to go down a small group of strings remains on the afterdeck to play the hymn *Nearer my God to thee* in the certainty that they will go down with the ship.

Only when the hymn has finished does Horner's own music take over – a series of pedals, rising in semitones and minor 3rds with chromatic brass chords above to add to the excitement. Much of this is obscured by sound effects of the ship sinking and the chaos and shouting as passengers rush for the lifeboats.

The song *My Heart Will Go On*, which was specially recorded by Celine Dion, is played during the final credits (it is never heard during the action). The film benefited from the success of this song as a chart single and James Horner ensured that it was related to the main body of the score by introducing it with the Irish melody that is played on the tin whistle throughout *Titanic*.

Television music

Finally, it is worth noting that Edexcel's list of genres mentioned earlier includes various types of music composed for television broadcasting. This is a reminder not to overlook the study of music for the small screen, in which musical ideas will not be quite as expansive and the instrumental resources will usually be more limited than in music intended to be heard in the cinema.

Studying this topic needs analytical and discriminating listening of your own favourite programmes. Remember that many of the more popular American sitcoms (such as *Friends* and *Ally McBeal*) have been issued on video and a cue from the score of *Inspector Morse* is included in the Edexcel *New Anthology of Music* (No. 46).

Words and Music

Remember that you should choose *either* 'Words and Music' or 'Music for the Moving Image' (see page 106) as your area of study.

This area of study (only applicable to A2) is the alternative to *Music for the Moving Image* and concerns the relationship between words and music, and how one can influence the other. In particular it requires you to be familiar with two specific albums, which will form the main focus of the second section of the Listening and Analysing paper. In addition, the *Words and Music* section of the composition briefs will usually include an assignment related to song, as we mentioned on page 92.

Composing

Listen to the following for interesting or unconventional ideas on how to approach your composition for 'Words and Music':
Reich: *Different Trains*; *Come Out*; *Tehilim*
Laurie Anderson: songs from *Big Science*
Jethro Tull: *Thick as a Brick*
Elvis Costello/Brodsky Quartet: *The Juliet Letters*

Useful websites about songwriting include:
http://www.craftofsongwriting.com/ and
http://www.euronet.nl/users/menke/
songs.html

Much of what you need to know has been covered in the Composing section of this book. Be aware, though, that before you begin your composition task, you will need to understand how words and music function together. The first step is to listen to the way other songwriters and composers have approached this. Listen to a range of vocal music covering songs from the last century and in a wide variety of styles from the standards of the 1920s, 1930s and 1940s to the work of Eminem and Tori Amos.

Don't be afraid to learn from other people! If an idea from a song you like works and you can use it in your own combination of words and music, this can only enhance your composition.

If the brief allows you to choose your own text you will need to consider whether to write your own lyrics or to use a poem or extract of prose. You will not be assessed on the quality of the lyrical content if you write your own words. Using this method, you may find that the words and music gel more easily, especially if you can use a lyric or text that particularly appeals to you.

Also, if the brief does not already include the text, you will need to decide if the words or the music should come first. Some people like to work with a well-structured lyric. This can help you to shape the music but it can also be restrictive. But if you start with music first you may have trouble fitting suitable words. There are pros and cons to both styles of working. One compromise adopted by songwriters is to work initially with a dummy lyric that will eventually be replaced – Paul McCartney's classic song *Yesterday* originally began life as: 'Scrambled eggs, oh, my baby, how I love your legs'!

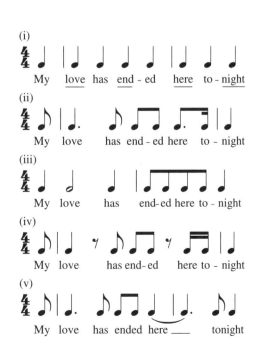

When setting words to music you will need to work out the scansion of the text – where the strong and weak accents fall – so that your music can support rather than work against the words. Some people prefer to do this by speaking the text aloud, underlining the stressed syllables and then fitting these to strong beats in the music. If you do this, be aware that you still have many choices to make. In the examples printed *left*, (i) shows a literal and rather boring alternation of strong and weak accents. The other rhythms are more varied: (ii) places the emphasis on 'love' by making it the longest note, (iii) stresses 'My' by positioning it on the first beat of the bar, (iv) introduces a breathless quality through the use of rests, while (v) accents 'here' by using syncopation to push its note earlier than expected. There are of course many other possibilities.

The brief may allow you to use words in a more general way, as a stimulus rather than as a specific text to be set to music. For instance, it could be that a descriptive passage in a novel or a poem conjures up musical ideas, visual images or textures. In cases such as this you should always ensure that the music can be directly related to the text you have chosen or been set.

You will need to decide on the style and form in which you intend to work. Depending on the brief, you could choose to use a straight-forward song format (intro, verse, chorus and so on) or you could decide to structure the piece in a more abstract way, using words simply for their sounds rather than as a means to communicate ideas.

You will also need to plan the technological resources and processes you intend to use – some ideas are listed on page 92. Remember that using spoken words, unusual sources and audio editing can help you to create an individual composition.

Listening and Analysing II

Edexcel has announced that for the 2006 and 2007 A2 exams, the *Words and Music* questions will be based on the following albums:

+ The Beach Boys: *Pet Sounds*
+ Marvin Gaye: *What's Going On*

You will need to know these two works in some detail. This will involve musical analysis in all the areas outlined below.

+ What is the melodic structure of each song?   **Melody and structure**
+ What is the range of its melody?
+ How does the melody reflect the words?
+ Are there climaxes and (literal) high points in the word-setting?
+ Is melismatic word-setting used to highlight particular words? For example

Music example from *You Still Believe Me* on *The Pet Sounds* album.

+ Are specific intervals stressed and used for a particular effect?
+ Is the phrasing regular?

+ Is the song major or minor?   **Tonality**
+ How does this help the communication of the lyric?
+ Are there contrasts of major/minor within the song and, if so, how do they influence the overall effect?

+ How has harmony been used and is it simple or complex?   **Harmony**
+ How does the harmony reflect the text?
+ How have cadences been used to help structure the song and enhance the lyric?
+ Have special chords been used to highlight certain words?

+ How has instrumentation been used in each song?   **Texture**
+ Are there any special effects (musical or technological) which stress or add weight to the words or to a musical phrase?

You will also need to be aware of other works by the same song-writers (leading up to, and progressing on from, the core albums) and from similar periods and related genres. This will involve getting to know the development of styles within the core albums: the expressive, vocal-based sounds of *Pet Sounds*, along with the creative arrangements and use of the studio, and Martin Gaye's development into a socially and politically aware artist. By listening to albums both before and after the focus works, you can gain an understanding of where the style came from and how it developed in terms of songwriting technique.

The Beach Boys: Pet Sounds

Availability

Pet Sounds was released as a mono album on vinyl in 1966. That original mono recording, remastered to CD, is currently available on EMI/Capitol 5273192. This is probably the best version to use for study. EMI/Capitol 5262662 includes the original mono tracks, a stereo remix that was created in the 1990s, and a bonus track (*Hang On To Your Ego*), all on the same CD. Capitol CDS 8376622 is a much more expensive four-CD set that includes mono and stereo mixes, alternate versions, out-takes, various *a capella* and instrumental-only mixes, and a 120-page book. Edexcel advises that questions will be set only on the material in the original version of the album.

The group

Useful websites about the Beach Boys:
www.beachboys.com/
www.thebeachboys.com
www.btinternet.com/~bellagio/
64.66.139.140/bbfclinx.htm

The Beach Boys (brothers Brian, Carl and Dennis Wilson, plus their cousin, Mike Love, and school friend, Alan Jardine) were the leading American pop group in the early 1960s. They built a reputation for irrepressibly cheerful songs about the 'sun and beach' lifestyle of their native California, particularly surfing, presented in sophisti-cated close-harmony arrangements made by eldest brother Brian. Their long string of international hits includes *Surfin' USA* (1963), *I Get Around* (1964), *Fun, Fun, Fun* (1964), *Help Me Rhonda* (1965), *California Girls* (1965), and *Good Vibrations* (1966).

The album

The innovative album *Pet Sounds* was released in 1966, and was the result of painstaking effort and constant reworking, rewriting and re-recording of material. It was a departure for both The Beach Boys in particular and for popular music in general, since until then albums were usually just a collection of unrelated tracks – a showcase of whatever songs happened to be ready for the market.

A **concept album** consists of a collection of songs written to lyrics that develop a single, often fictional idea through each successive track, as in the Beatles' Sergeant Pepper's Lonely Hearts Club Band (1967). *Pet Sounds* is not itself a concept album, but is a key step in that direction, with its gradually emerging theme of the hopes, dreams and fears felt by young people as they approach adulthood.

Pet Sounds was not particularly a search for commercial success but more a search for artistic freedom and expression. The Beatles were on a similar musical path at this time, and their studio album *Rubber Soul* (1965) was an important influence on Brian Wilson, who said 'It felt like it all belonged together. *Rubber Soul* was a collection of songs ... that somehow went together like no album ever made before, and I was very impressed'. Paul McCartney later returned the compliment, acknowledging that '*Pet Sounds* was my inspiration for making *Sgt. Pepper* ... the big influence'.

Today some of the lyrics of *Pet Sounds* may seem a little naive, but there is an honest and open simplicity about the album that has an extremely immediate quality. It retains some elements from the surf-pop albums the band had released previously, including lyrics about teenage romance, but the lyrical and musical context is altogether more sophisticated and more highly developed than that of their early hits. One only has to listen to *Surfin' Safari*, the band's first album (released in 1962), to hear how far they had moved away from their essentially rock 'n' roll roots (listen to *Little Miss America* and *Honky Tonk* from *Surfin' Safari*, for example).

Some of the tracks on *Pet Sounds* retain the uplifting 'feel good' quality established by The Beach Boys in their earlier hits, but there are also more introspective songs, such as *God Only Knows* and *Caroline, No*, which reflect the growing maturity of the band and in particular the songwriting skills of Brian Wilson and his new-found lyricist Tony Asher. The arrangements and the production skills used to create the recordings of these songs also show a high level of expertise and craftsmanship.

Lyrically, the songs deal with love, relationships, growing up, self-discovery and … sailing. The love songs are often reflective and wistful in character, rather than exuding the uninhibited joy of previous hits such as *Help Me Rhonda*, *Good Vibrations* and *California Girls*.

The opening track, *Wouldn't It Be Nice*, gets the album off to a flying start with what was to become a Beach Boys' standard. The intro beguilingly sets up a gentle chord pattern in A major on the harp – but after a sudden rim-shot from the snare drum, the key plummets down a third to F major for the first verse, with its chugging rhythms and high, close harmonies that are such a trademark of Brian Wilson's work. Mike Love takes over the lead vocal for the bridge ('Maybe if we think and wish and hope and pray it might come true …'), the change of key and the return of the harp, not only providing contrast but also harking back to the texture of the intro. At the end of the bridge a link is formed from four bars of tonic chord featuring a prominent *ritardando* (slowing up) that leads to a much slower tempo for the truncated third verse. This innovative treatment clearly reflects the melancholy turn in the lyric just before the end ('You know it seems the more we talk about it, it only makes it worse to live without it').

The second track is a beautifully-crafted ballad, *You Still Believe in Me*. The harmony is based on a simple three-chord pattern heard three times in the intro, six times in the first half of both verses, and many times more in the outro. But the second half of each verse ends with a most unexpected chord (on the flattened 6th of the scale – G major in the key of B major), reflecting the wonder of the singer ('How can it be, you still believe in me?'). The beautiful melismatic phrase that is repeated to bring this haunting song to a close ('I wanna cry') is shown on page 123.

That's Not Me is another example of the way in which the Beach Boys (or more properly, Brian Wilson) use texture to reflect changes of mood. Listen to the way the texture changes for the sections beginning 'I'm a little bit scared' and 'I once had a dream'. The strong percussive elements drop out to leave a smooth, sustained organ and vocal texture with a heavily reverbed guitar. This song has no intro, but notice how unusual harmonic twists give variety to what might otherwise be a rather repetitive verse structure.

The tracks

For background information, see:
www.beachboysfanclub.com/ps-liner.html
www.beachboysfanclub.com/ps-tracks.html

The plucked sound in the intro was produced by plucking the strings of a piano with paper clips, hairpins and other objects. The sounds of a bicycle bell near the end of verse two and a horn in the outro occur because the song was originally intended to be about childhood – it was too late to change the backing when the decision was taken to record a different vocal solo.

The slow tempo and static accompaniment of *Don't Talk (Put Your Head on my Shoulder)*, the second ballad on the album, has a languid stillness that reflects its lyrics. The first verse begins with a very sparse texture, allowing Brian Wilson's double-tracked solo vocal to come to the fore. Almost imperceptibly, accompanying parts gradually introduce a little more movement, propelling the second verse to its emotional climax – 'Listen to my heart beat … listen, listen, listen'. And as the bass guitar mimics the beating heart, the singer is overwhelmed by a glorious string overdub, its conclusion signalled by a short timpani rhythm and leading to a fade-out based on repetitions of the hypnotic two-bar chord pattern from the start of the chorus:

(Original one semitone higher)

Don't talk, ___ put your head ___ on my shoul - der,

This song was written in 1964, well before the rest of *Pet Sounds*. However, even though it may have been 'drafted in' to complete the album, commentators seem agreed that it fits into the overall style and direction of the project.

I'm Waiting for the Day restores an up-beat mood with its rousing opening for timpani and drum kit, followed by the distinctive sound of the electric organ played staccato. The style quickly becomes more relaxed as the accompaniment thins out for the vocal entry, but the rather eccentric, galloping percussion return for the second verse – only to exit again for the second chorus, which has a more relaxed, sustained mood to match the lyrics ('He hurt you then, but that's all gone').

Once again, vivid contrasts of texture can be heard to form a key feature of this album. Brian Wilson underlines this in his lead vocal by switching from the pleading tone of verse one to an aggresive verse two ('I kissed your lips … it made me think about him'), then back to a nonchalant account of the second chorus, and finally to an almost manic fury for the outro (the inward-looking nature of which is emphasised by unrelieved tonic harmony throughout).

Let's Go Away For A While is mellow and warm, but as one of two solely instrumental tracks on the album it doesn't really belong to your 'words and music' area of study, and so you should not expect questions on it. However, the inclusion of purely instrumental music was in itself an innovative feature of a pop album at this time, and it forms an interesting arrangement, particularly with its changes of texture and sometimes quirky use of percussion.

The *Sloop John B* is a folksong (or more precisely a sea shanty) about a wild party that had reputedly followed the sinking of a sloop (a type of sailing ship designed to carry cargo) in the harbour at Nassau in the Bahamas in the early 20th century. The song first appeared in print in 1927 and had been recorded by a number of different folk singers and folk groups before it became a hit for The Beach Boys.

The words and melody of *Sloop John B* come from a traditional folk song (see *left*). The inclusion of folk music in an album of otherwise original material was unusual, and it can be argued that the lyrics don't rest comfortably with those of the other tracks. However, the repetitive nature of the song and its simple harmonic basis (using only four basic chords) lend themselves to Brian Wilson's style of arrangement, with its glittering glockenspiel and increasingly elaborate vocal writing as the song progresses – notice particularly the *a cappella* section at 1'50", where we hear only unaccompanied part-singing in a stunning change of texture. The lively tempo and repetitive verse-and-chorus structure give the song a sing-along quality that helped make it (along with *Wouldn't it be Nice* and *God Only Knows*) one of three worldwide top-ten hits from the album.

Said to be Paul McCartney's favourite song, *God Only Knows* is a melancholy love song, full of musical subtleties. The lead vocal is sung by Carl Wilson and the harmony is frequently elusive – the bass is seldom on the root of the current chord, and the avoidance of the tonic in the bass often leaves the key seeming ambivalent.

The instrumentation, too, is particularly unusual. The melody in the intro is played by an orchestral horn – notice the upward *glissando* (slide) in bars 2 and 6 and the harpsichord accompaniment (joined by jingle bells in bar 5). The sound (rather like horses' hooves) at the start of the first verse is produced by coconut shells. The instrumental break after verse 2 starts with a melody on *pizzicato* (plucked) strings, accompanied by staccato chords on an electric organ. It leads to a break verse and chorus which most unusually is a 4th (five semitones) higher than the previous verses. It is sung to nonsense syllables (a style known as scat singing) and leads to a repeat of verse 2 back in its original key. Once again, strong contrasts, particularly in the instrumental interludes, form an important feature of the album.

The hook ('God only knows what I'd be without you') at the end of the chorus is developed into a beautiful coda to end the song – as one voice ends on 'you' the next starts the hook, with an overlap that makes it sound like the start of a round. This musical imitation is then intensified by starting the overlap earlier in the hook (after 'God only knows what I'd') and introducing variations and descants – and soon, what could so easily have been a boringly repetitive fadeout swells into an outpouring of vocal polyphony.

The intro of *I Know There's an Answer* is enlivened by the entry of a bass harmonica halfway through. All of the music is based on just two chords until after the words 'safety zones' – at which point the music plunges from B♭ major to D♭ major, winding its way back to B♭ in time for the chorus. The second verse and chorus follow the pattern of the first, but the third verse starts as an instrumental (listen out for the banjo accompanying the bass harmonica), the voices not entering until the distinctive modulation. This type of stub section of a verse is sometimes known as a pre-chorus. The outro is based on the same two-chord pattern as the intro.

This song initially had the title *Hang on to your Ego*, and different words in the chorus. This early version, which is included as a bonus track on some CDs of *Pet Sounds*, was considered to refer too overtly to drugs, especially since Brian Wilson was starting to experiment with the psychedelic drugs to which he would sadly become addicted.

Track 10, *Here Today*, is a forceful song, matching lyrics that are essentially warnings from a former boyfriend about the dangers of love. The catalogue of woe ('It makes you feel so bad, it makes your heart feel sad, it makes your days go wrong, it makes your nights so long') is driven home by treating each statement as a musical sequence. Heavy drums and thick scoring underline the point – 'Love is here today and it's gone tomorrow'. Notice how this lyric crosses what would normally be a clear divide between verse and chorus – the latter starts at 'Here today', and is built over repetitions of a gloomily descending bass line (G, F♯, F♮, E, D).

The instrumental break that replaces the third verse features a characteristic 1960s sound – rapidly repeated pitches on the bass guitar. Above this, the accompaniment consists of isolated chords (sometimes referred to as 'stop' style) that allow the bass to retain the focus. However, the most remarkable thing about this section is the background studio chatter that was clearly deliberately left in for the final release of the album. It includes a conversation about cameras and the voice of Brian Wilson saying 'Top, please' (an instruction to start again from the beginning). This moment of whimsy was to be mirrored by the Beatles when they decided to end *Sgt. Pepper* with background sounds from the album's post-production party.

I Just Wasn't Made For These Times returns to a melancholy style, reflected in Brian Wilson's impassioned vocal delivery. Wilson later indicated that the song was a personal statement, expressing his feeling that he didn't fit in with society. Notice how the chorus constantly returns to a B minor chord – although it includes some of Wilson's typical harmonic fluidity, it is essentially based in the dorian mode on B (B, C♯, D, E, F♯, G♯, A), accentuating the despondent three-fold repetition of 'Sometimes I feel very sad'. Notice, too, how the word 'wrong' is poignantly buried in the mix on the line 'But what goes wrong' and how the words of the backing vocals are deliberately driven into obscurity, almost like voices 'heard in the head' ('Ain't found the one thing I can put my heart and soul into' and 'My friends don't know or want me').

The instrumental break includes a part for an early electronic instrument called a thérémin (see page 14). This was probably its first ever use in pop music, although it was to feature much more extensively in The Beach Boy's most famous hit, *Good Vibrations* (1966).

Track 12, *Pet Sounds*, is another purely instrumental track. Wilson rather enigmatically said it was supposed to resemble the type of theme tune used in James Bond movies. The unique percussion sound was produced by the drummer playing two empty Coca-Cola cans – yet another idea from Brian Wilson's fertile imagination.

Wilson said that the final track, *Caroline, No*, was about growing up and the loss of innocence (thus perhaps confirming the overall concept of the album) – a nostalgic plea to return to earlier days and to ignore the reality of the here and now. It is a bitter-sweet ballad featuring Brian Wilson alone (the solo is double-tracked), without any vocal backing. The track opens with a rhythm tapped on an empty soda-syphon bottle, followed by echoed bongo drums, and ends with extraneous sounds (a passing train and the barking of Wilson's dogs) – perhaps as a sort or reminder of the 'outside world'.

As written, the key of the song is effectively F major, but this is constantly obscured by the frequent chords of G, which contain B♮. However, *Caroline, No* sounds a semitone higher than indicated here, because before the final release the decision was taken to slightly speed up the tape of this song in order to brighten the tone of the vocal.

The tiny percussive intro is followed by three verses and an outro, all based on the same chord pattern, with a contrasting bridge between verses two and three. The principal chord pattern is based largely on the alternation of two adjacent chords, G and F, with frequent added 6ths and 7ths, setting up a typical ambivalence of key and underlining the yearning and sense of homelessness in the song. These harmonies are outlined as broken chords (i.e. patterns of separate notes) on the harpsichord.

Notice the change in the vocal at the end of verse 3, to create a more impassioned final exclamation of 'Oh Caroline no'. This leads into the outro, where the horn takes over the vocal melody, almost as if the singer cannot finds words to finish the song.

Other Listening

Some features of *Pet Sounds* look back to the 'surf music' of the early 1960s and others look forward to some of the more surreal and innovative elements of psychedelic rock. Other albums to look out for include:

✦ *All Time Greatest Hits* by Jan and Dean

Brian Wilson co-wrote some of the songs performed by this surfing duo – note the similarity of vocal harmony style, the chugging rhythms and 'summer fun' feel on tracks such as *Surf City*, *Little Old Lady (from Pasadena)* and *Baby Talk*.

Available on CD from Curb Records, IMP 77374-2

✦ *Rubber Soul* by The Beatles

This album was an influence on, and a starting point for, Brian Wilson in creating *Pet Sounds*. If you don't already know it, also make a point of listening to *Sgt. Pepper's Lonely Hearts Club Band*.

CDs of these two albums are available on Parlophone CDP746440-2 and CDP 746442-2 respectively.

✦ *Da Capo* by Love

Love was a West Coast folk-rock/psychedelic band that didn't last long, but this album probably shows them at their psychedelic best, particularly on the track *Orange Skies*.

Available on CD from Rhino, 8122-73604-2.

Private Study

Listen to The Beach Boys' 1966 hit, *Good Vibrations* (available on numerous compilations) and compare it with *I'm Waiting for the Day* from *Pet Sounds*.

1. What are the similarities in the arrangements of these two songs?

2. What makes *Good Vibrations* a hit single while *I'm Waiting for the Day* is more clearly an album track?

Listen to *Help Me Rhonda* from The Beach Boys' 1965 album, *Today!*

3. Which musical elements of this song can also be found in the music on *Pet Sounds*?

4. How has The Beach Boys' use of harmony changed on the *Pet Sounds* album?

Listen to the track *Be Still* from The Beach Boys's 1968 album, *Friends*. Brian Wilson was no longer the main writer for the group and this song was written by Dennis Wilson and Steve Kalinich.

5. What stylistic features identify this as a Beach Boys' song despite it not being written by Brian Wilson?

6. What features (stylistic, performance and production) make it clear that this song is *not* written, arranged and produced by Brian Wilson?

Marvin Gaye: What's Going On

Availability

What's Going On was released on vinyl in 1971 and is available on CD from Motown, 530022-2 – it has nine tracks. The 'Original Recording Remastered' CD from Island (064022-2) includes the original nine tracks plus two bonus tracks. The two-CD 'Deluxe Edition' (Universal 013404-2) has 35 tracks, and contains various alternative mixes and live versions. Edexcel has announced that questions will only be set on the original nine tracks.

Martin Gaye

See page 29 for more on gospel and page 31 for more on soul.

Websites offering information about Marvin Gaye include:

www.icebergradio.com/artist/4344/
    marvin_gaye.html

www.soulwalking.co.uk/
    Marvin%20Gaye.html

marvingayepage.cjb.net/

Motown developed in the early 1960s as a sophisticated style of pop music, influenced by soul and by the call-and-response vocals of gospel, and frequently presented in elaborate arrangements that included orchestral strings along with jazz-like saxophone and brass sections.

Marvin Gaye was Motown's best-selling male artist – he had a wide vocal range and could tackle styles ranging from jazz ballads, rhythm 'n' blues and hot gospel, to smooth love songs. He had a string of solo hits, from the early *Stubborn Kind Of Fellow* (1962) to such all-time greats as *How Sweet it is to be Loved by You* (1964) and *I Heard it Through the Grapevine* (1968). He also scored huge success as a duet artist, firstly with Mary Wells and later, and even more successfully, with Tammi Terrell until her death in 1970 from a brain tumour. Gaye's own life came to a tragic end in 1984, when he was shot by his father after a series of bitter arguments.

The album

During the 1960s, Marvin Gaye had mainly focused on Motown-orientated dance music or romantic ballads. His self-produced 1971 album *What's Going On* proved to be a turning point for Gaye as an artist and an inspiration for a new generation of rhythm 'n' blues performers. His lyrics, embracing subjects such as poverty, war and politics, became more spiritually and socially aware following the death of Terrell and the return of his brother from Vietnam. At the same time, his musical arrangements became (with the help of the Funk Brothers) tinged with jazz flavours, creating a distinctive new sound. Marvin Gaye not only performs the lead vocal but also exploits the still relatively new technique of multi-tracking in order to sing his own backing vocals.

Motown was, at first, unwilling to release this material but the fact that this album went on to become his best-selling solo album, spawning three chart-topping singles (*What's Going On, Mercy Mercy Me (The Ecology)*, and *Inner City Blues*) proved the company wrong. The album also influenced Motown and rhythm 'n' blues artists such as Stevie Wonder, allowing them to challenge beliefs through an accessible medium.

The tracks

The title track, *What's Going On*, opens the album with a taste of what is to come: mellow, jazz-tinged rhythm 'n' blues. Gaye's restrained vocal belies the passion of the lyric, which is concerned with all kinds of social ills from war and poverty to racial bigotry. Note that there is no question mark in the title – it is a statement of what is going on, not a query. The detachment of Gaye's voice from the background sounds of a party seems to emphasise how concern for the trivia of our own existence blinds our attention to the types of global issues that are as relevant today as they were 35 years ago when this track was created. By using a restrained delivery, Gaye homes in on the positive message that only love can conquer hate. The title is repeated as the chorus to reinforce the message that the status quo should be challenged.

This first track segues into *What's Happening Brother*, starting the succession of continuous music that continues until the end of track 6. It uses an innovative groove which, unusually for Motown, features prominent jazz-flavoured congas, Latin percussion and finger clicks. This time there *is* a question implied by the title, since the lyrics provide an answer in the form of an account from a soldier returning from the war in Vietnam (as did Gaye's brother). A wordless vocal segues us into the next track.

Segue (pronounced 'seg-way') is an Italian word meaning 'follows'. In music it is used to indicate that the next item should follow without a break.

The lyric of *Flying High in the Empty Sky* deals with drug abuse – its dangers and its attractions – possibly as a reaction to the many drug-dependant Vietnam veterans, although ironically its was to be Marvin Gaye's own drug abuse that contributed to the tragedy of his own death at the hands of his father. The opening is quite dramatic in its use of percussion, but musically the rest of the song feels quite unstructured and wandering, perhaps reflecting the thoughts of a junkie. Marvin Gaye's vocal style is impassioned and soulful, particularly on the phrase 'the pain, oh the pain'.

Save the Children turns to the idea of the failing ecology and the future of the human race. Musically, there are conflicting ideas: the floating strings, the child-like glockenspiel and the driving conga rhythm. Similarly there are spoken vocals and those that are sung: the former quite laid-back, the latter most heated. The song builds to a climax for the fervent phrase 'save the babies' and concludes with a coda (at 3'13") in the same tempo as the next track, into which it segues, demonstrating that the album was conceived to be listened to as a whole rather than as separate songs.

Diana Ross recorded a cover version of *Save the Children* for her 1973 album, *Touch me in the Morning*. She also recorded an album jointly with Marvin Gaye that same year.

Track 5, *God Is Love*, is a short, joyous song using multi-tracked vocals to create a call-and-response structure with a very gospel-based feel.

Mercy Mercy Me (The Ecology) has an upbeat yet mellow feel, with its lush strings, radio-friendly hook, laid-back vocal delivery and warm production, all of which contrast strongly with the somewhat depressing lyric ('animals and birds who live nearby are dying'). The hook, unusually, is in the first line of each of the short verses as there is no chorus. Listen carefully to this track and see if you can spot that the underlying harmony consists of just four chords, everyone of which contains a 7th – E^{maj7}, $C\sharp m^7$, $F\sharp m^7$, A^{maj7}. It is these constant 7ths, which occur in the melody and many of the backing parts, that produce the warmth of Gaye's soft-hued style. Equally important is the bass which, in total contrast, keeps almost entirely to the root and 5th of each chord, repeating notes in order to give rhythmic impetus to the slow changes of the basic chord pattern. The long coda, with its saxophone improvisation and curious ending, concludes not only this song but also the entire succession of six linked tracks that formed the first side of the original vinyl album. Its melancholy tone seems to offer a chance for wordless reflection on the lyrics that have preceeded it.

Notice how the phrase 'Love can conquer hate' from the lyrics of the title track appears again in this song at 6'05" – compare the two uses of these words.

Aretha Franklin included a cover version of *Wholly Holy* in her 1972 album of gospel and other religious music, *Amazing Grace*.

Right On is a Latin jazz workout, featuring the scraping sound of the guiro on the first and third beats, as well as cowbell and conga, plus an improvisatory line played on the flute. Its is based on a single riff worked through three chords until 4'59" where, at the words 'love, love, sweet love', the mood changes to a more laid-back style for a while until the jubilant Latin mood takes over again. The vocal throughout is improvisatory in nature, revealing the honest and sincere nature of the lyric.

The penultimate track, *Wholly Holy*, has a very spiritual quality with its lack of drums and repetition of the words 'wholly holy' (which are homonyms – words that sound the same but that are spelled differently). There is, again, a gospel flavour to this track with an effect of call-and-response between the lead and backing vocals. The simplicity of the words is reflected in the simple presentation of the music.

Inner City Blues (Make Me Wanna Holler) features another soulful vocal performance. There are no blues elements in the music – the term 'blues' in the title refers to the nature of the lyrics ('this ain't livin'') and the impassioned vocal delivery. The harmony is exceptionally static, allowing the lyric and the vocal to shine through. Marvin Gaye ends the song with a look back to the opening track of the album ('Mother, mother, everybody thinks we're wrong'). This brief reprise gives a cyclical quality to the entire album, making it seem almost like a song cycle or a kind of concept album.

What's Going On became one of the most memorable soul albums of all time. Part of the reason for this is undoubtedly the sheer expressive range of Marvin Gaye's singing, which brings out every nuance in the lyrics. His style has its roots in both soul music and jazz, and an important part of his technique is the use of *rubato* ('robbed time') in which he sometimes pushes fractionally ahead of the beat, or deliberately delays notes fractionally behind the beat, in order to place emphasis on certain notes and, thereby, on important words. This frees up the rhythm and allows the vocal line to mimic spoken speech patterns more closely, allowing for greater expression. This can be clearly heard in *Flyin' High*, where Gaye also uses *falsetto* (a singing technique that produces sounds above the singer's normal range) to great effect, both in terms of making a frail, submissive sound and in creating a despairing wail.

Throughout the album, Marvin Gaye uses a great range of vocal timbre, constantly changing to express the qualities and ideas behind the lyric. Listen to the way he uses lyrics in *Save the Children* – compare the spoken portion of the lyric with the sung words. What words and phrases does he emphasise, and how?

Other Listening

Marvin Gaye's *What's Going On* is a beautiful example of post-Motown soul, but it is also an example of politically and socially aware songwriting. Other examples include:

✦ *Songs in the Key of Life* by Stevie Wonder

Stevie Wonder, another Motown artist, made this album in 1976 and there are clear links to Gaye's seminal work both in terms of soundscapes and lyrical content. Check out *Love's in Need of Love Today*, *Have a Talk With God*, *Village Ghetto Land*, *Pastime Paradise* and *Black Man*.

Available as a bargain-priced two-CD set on Motown 157357-2.

✦ *The Freewheelin' Bob Dylan* by Bob Dylan

While this folky album of 1963 is in a very different musical style, the social awareness and political stance of some of the songs (*A Hard Rain's Gonna Fall*, *Blowin' in the Wind*, *Masters of War* and *Oxford Town*) are not dissimilar to those of Gaye's.

Available on Columbia 512348-2.

✦ *You're All I Need* by Marvin Gaye and Tammi Terrell

This 1968 album is an example of Gaye's work immediately prior to *What's Going On* – the content is somewhat different both lyrically and musically, and has a much more sugary flavour.

Available on Motown 013217-2.

Private Study

Listen to Marvin Gaye's 1964 single *How Sweet It Is (To Be Loved By You)* (it can be found on the CD *The Very Best Of Marvin Gaye*) and *God Is Love* from *What's Going On*.

1. What differences are there in terms of harmony, melody and song structure?

Listen to the song *You Sure Love to Ball* from Gaye's 1973 album, *Let's Get It On*.

2. What elements of this song are heard in *What's Going On*?

3. How has Gaye's lyrical direction changed in the 1973 song?

Listen to the 1982 track *Sexual Healing*, which can also be found on the CD *The Very Best Of Marvin Gaye*.

4. Describe both the old-style Gaye elements heard on this track, and the new influences that you hear.

5. How is Gaye using technology to enhance his musical ideas in this song?

Glossary

Accidental. A symbol in front of a note that indicates a change of pitch from the expected note. Accidentals include the sharp (♯) to indicate raising the note by a semitone and the flat (♭) to indicate lowering it by a semitone. The natural (♮) indicates that the note should be neither sharpened nor flattened.

ADT. Automatic double tracking. Emulates the effect of recording a musician playing the same thing twice on two separate tracks. It uses a short **delay** to simulate the timing discrepancies.

Aftertouch. The pressure applied to a keyboard key after it has been struck. This is transmitted by a specific MIDI message.

Ambient. A recording made with microphones carefully placed around the auditorium. Thus what is recorded is the sound of the instruments and the processing effect of the space – if an audience is present any sounds they make get recorded too! Sometimes used as the opposite of **close-mic** techniques.

Amplified. Put through an amplifier (amp). Informally the term is often used to mean making a sound louder, but this it not necessarily the case.

Amplitude. The relative strength of a sound wave or electric signal. If the amplitude of a wave increases it will sound louder.

Analogue. Refers to a signal that directly represents variable data (such as sound or video images), as opposed to **digital** in which such signals are represented by a stream of numbers. Analogue recording media (such as records or cassettes) store the sound using a continuously varying signal.

Articulation. The amount of separation between successive notes. If there are no gaps the music is **legato**, while if notes are shortened to leave gaps between them, it is **staccato**. The attack and dynamic of each note also play a role in the articulation of music.

Audio. Sound or hearing. Often used in the expression 'audio signal', referring to an electrical signal that uses variations (eg in voltage) to convey information that can be converted to sound by a loudspeaker.

Balance. The relative volume levels between instruments.

Bank change. A MIDI controller message type, which switches a MIDI instrument to a different bank of sounds. It is usually followed by a program change message to select a sound from the new bank.

Bouncing. The process of mixing-down material from several tracks and re-recording it on one (or two) new tracks, in order to free up more tracks on a multitrack tape.

bpm. Beats per minute. Refers to the tempo of a piece. If there are 60 beats per minute (60 bpm) there will be one beat per second. 120 bpm is twice as fast – one beat every half-second.

Call-and-response. The performance of alternate musical phrases by different soloists or groups, so that one seems to answer the other (known in art music as antiphony).

Canon. A musical device (sometimes an entire piece) in which a melody in one part fits with the same melody in another part even though the latter starts a few beats later. The device occurs in the type of song known as a round.

CD. Compact disc. A popular **digital** recording format. It first appeared in 1982 and by 1988 sales of CDs were already surpassing sales of vinyl records.

CD-ROM. Compact Disc Read-Only Memory. A digital data storage format, based on the same technology as the CD. It is used to store and distribute up to 700MB of computer files.

Chord. A combination of notes played at the same time to create harmony. Often denoted by symbols, eg Cm, $F\sharp^7$.

Chorus. (1) A section of a song which returns several times. (2) A group of singers. (3) An electronic effect used to thicken a sound by combining slightly altered versions of sound with the original signal. (4) MIDI controller 93, which is used to adjust the chorus (thickening) level applied to a sound.

Chromatic. Notes outside the current key, that are used for their colour rather than for **modulation**.

Clef. A musical symbol, appearing at the start of each line of printed music, denoting the range of pitches on the stave. The commonest (seen in piano music) are the treble and bass clefs. However there are other clefs, eg the alto (for viola) and tenor (for the upper registers of cello and bassoon music).

The same note (middle C) in four different clefs

Treble clef   Bass clef   Alto clef   Tenor clef

Close-mic. The art of recording singers or instruments with the microphone very close to the sound source. In this way many extra details are picked up (eg the breath of a singer or the string noise of a guitar) and the playing can be quieter and more intimate. Producers can also have greater control in the final balance than is possible in an **ambient** recording.

Coincident pair. A stereo microphone technique in which two separate microphones are placed so that their diaphragms occupy approximately the same point in space. They are angled apart and placed so that one is directly on top of the other. Also known as a crossed pair.

Compressor. An audio effect that reduces the range of volume of a sound. Producers use it to even out the balance when recording instruments and voices whose dynamics vary greatly. Guitarists use this effect to produce a more even solo sound. Compressors are also regularly used when broadcasting, say, classical music so that people in cars can still hear a solo flute at the same volume setting as an entire orchestra.

Condenser microphone. A microphone that works on the principle of variable capacitance to generate an electrical signal.

Contrapuntal. Music that uses counterpoint – ie two or more simultaneous melodies with independent rhythms.

Controller. (1) A MIDI input device such as a keyboard or electronic wind instrument. (2) A type of MIDI message, which can be used for controlling aspects of the sound such as volume or reverb.

DAT. Digital Audio Tape. A tape-based digital recording medium, introduced in 1987 and still mostly used in studios.

Data. Information. Data can take different forms such as audio, video, MIDI and text.

Delay. An effect which produces a copy of the input sound signal, which lags behind the input by a specified amount. Delay is used as an effect in its own right, but it is also a component of **ADT**, **chorus**, **flange** and **phasing**.

DI (direct injection). The direct connection of an electric instrument such as a bass guitar to a mixing desk. This is often done via a DI box which matches the electrical characteristics of the source signal to the input level required.

Digital. Refers to a signal which is encoded as numbers. When sound is digitised, the original **analogue** signal is represented by a stream of numbers, and can thus be stored in, and manipulated by, a computer system.

Distortion. The rough (or dirty) sound produced when an audio signal is deformed. It can result from poor electronic components, faulty leads or amplifier levels set too high – but it is also sometimes used deliberately as an electric-guitar effect.

Download. To obtain information (eg from the Internet or from a disk) by transferring it onto your own computer system.

Double tracking. The process of recording two different performances of the same material to thicken a musical line. See also **ADT**.

Drum machine. A device that offers a range of synthesised and/or sampled percussion sounds, and the means to sequence them into rhythm patterns.

DVD. Digital Versatile Disc. A high-density recording medium, introduced in 1996, used for films and computer data storage.

Dynamic microphone. A microphone that generates an electrical signal when acoustic pressure waves cause a conductive coil to vibrate in a stationary magnetic field.

Dynamics. The degree of loudness in music. This is indicated in scores by symbols such as $\boldsymbol{p}$ (*piano* = quiet), $\boldsymbol{f}$ (*forte* = loud) and ⟍ (*crescendo* = gradually increasing in loudness).

Echo. The effect of a **delay** long enough (eg greater than ¼ second) to produce a distinct copy of the sound.

Editing. The art of manipulating data (such as a computer file or recording) in order to improve it or to produce something different. Editing a recording originally involved splicing and looping bits of tape, but nowadays it is mostly done with digital processing.

Effects. A term used to describe a variety of sound processing techniques such as **reverb**, **delay**, **chorus**, **flange** and **phasing**. It also commonly refers to devices which carry out these tasks.

Electret. A type of **condenser microphone** in which the electrostatic charge on the plates of the capacitor is generated by an electret – a material that permanently stores an electrostatic charge.

Elektronische Musik. A style of composition originating in Cologne in the early 1950s, using electronic synthesised sounds.

Envelope. The shape of a synthesised note's amplitude (eg how fast the note starts its attack, and how long it takes to decay).

EQ. Equalisation. Any control that adjusts the relative frequency components of a sound, such as tone controls (treble, mid, bass).

Flange. A sweeping **delay** effect in which the delay-time is continuously changing. The name originates from the flange on the outside of a tape reel, which if pressed by an engineer varied the speed of the playback with respect to another, identical reel.

Floppy disk. A small removable data storage device found on most computer systems. Typically stores up to 1.4MB (megabytes).

Foldback. An audio signal sent from the mixer to the studio area for replay to the performers (usually on headphones).

Frequency. The number of times per second that a sound wave or electrical voltage oscillates. The higher the frequency of a sound the higher its perceived pitch. Doubling the frequency has the effect of raising the pitch of a note by an octave (see *right*). Frequency used to be measured in cycles per second (CPS) but is now more commonly expressed in Hertz (Hz).

A
440 Hz

A
880 Hz

FX. An abbreviation of **effects**.

Gate. A device for letting a sound through only when it is above a specified volume threshold. Used in recording to reduce background noise when an instrument is not playing.

Genre. A category or type of music, such as dance music, vocal music or opera.

GM. General MIDI. An extension to the MIDI specification, which standardises sounds and controllers.

Hard disk. A large-capacity data storage device for computers. Unlike a **floppy disk** it is not normally removeable.

Headphones. Basically a pair of **loudspeakers** small enough to fit over the ears so that sounds can be heard by an individual with minimal disturbance to others in the vicinity.

Hemiola. A rhythmic device in which two groups of three beats are articulated as three groups of two beats (see *right*) causing a type of **syncopation**. The device is common at cadences in triple-time baroque music.

Hi-fi. Short for high fidelity. Refers to good-quality sound, and the equipment that provides it.

Hook. A short melodic idea in pop music that is designed to be instantly memorable.

Key signature. A set of sharps or flats that determines which key the following music is to be played in (although **accidentals** within the course of the music may change that key).

Legato. Smooth. A musical line without gaps between notes, often shown in music notation by a curved line above or below the notes affected. The opposite of **staccato**.

Lo-fi. Low fidelity. Often used to denote the intentional lowering of sound quality to achieve a particular musical effect.

Loudspeaker. A device which converts electrical audio signals into changes in air pressure, so that the signals can be perceived as sound.

MD. Mini-disc. A digital recording format similar to CD, but with a 7cm disc, introduced in 1993.

Metronome. A mechanical or electronic device which produces a click or beep at a regular and adjustable rate in order to determine a tempo and regular pulse for music. A metronome mark of ♩=60 (or MM=60) is the same as 60bpm and means one beat per second.

Microphone (often abbreviated to 'mic', and pronounced and sometimes written as 'mike'). A device to convert the rapid changes in air pressure caused by sound into electrical signals that can be recorded, amplified or processed in various ways before being converted back into the audio domain by loudspeakers.

MIDI. Musical Instrument Digital Interface. A standard for connecting and remotely operating electronic instruments and related devices such as computers and effects units.

MIDI channel. One of 16 possible instrumental tracks of data that can be accommodated from a single **MIDI port**.

MIDI file. A computer data file which stores sequences of MIDI information.

MIDI port. A device in (or attached to) a computer which allows it to communicate with MIDI instruments.

Mixing. The art of blending together separate audio tracks. This may include adjusting their **balance**, **stereo panning** and **EQ**, as well as adding **effects**.

Mixing desk. A device for processing, combining and monitoring audio signals, usually with a view to producing a final two-channel (stereo) output.

Modulation. (1) A musical term for a change of key. (2) A technical term relating to one signal being modified by another, often when a sound is altered in pitch by another waveform. (3) A MIDI controller message type 1, which controls the amount of vibrato.

Monitor. (1) To listen to (or measure) an audio signal, either via headphones or via monitor speakers. (2) The visual display unit (VDU or screen) used in a computer or video system.

Mono. An audio signal carried by a single channel. All records from before 1958 (and tapes before 1954) were in mono.

Monophonic. (1) A term used to describe instruments that can play only one note at a time. Early synthesisers were monophonic. (2) Music that consists of only one note at a time, such as an unaccompanied melody.

MTC (MIDI Time Code). An extension to the **MIDI** specification that allows time (in hours, minutes, seconds and frames) to be transmitted, enabling synchronisation with **SMPTE** devices.

Multi-timbral. Capable of playing several timbres at once.

Multitrack. A recording technique where several tracks of sound are recorded independently but can be played back together.

Musique concrète. A style of composition, originating in Paris in the late 1940s, which manipulated recorded sounds.

Muted. (1) An instruction to an instrumentalist (*con sordino* in Italian) to use a mute to muffle the sound. (2) The temporary silencing of a recorded audio track.

Note On. A MIDI message denoting the onset of a note.

Normalisation. An offline digital process where the amplitude of the recorded signal is multiplied to make use of the full dynamic range of the digital recording medium.

Ornament. Decorative notes (sometimes called grace notes) that embellish a main note. In scores they may be written out in full or indicated by a special symbol. Or they may be improvised in some styles of music. Common ornaments are the trill, mordent, turn, acciaccatura and appoggiatura.

Oscillate. To vibrate regularly, and thus have the potential for making sound.

Ostinato. A musical idea or phrase which repeats for a substantial time. In pop and jazz this is often called a **riff**.

Overdub. The process of recording a new musical part on an unused track in synchronisation with previously recorded tracks.

Panning. The placing of a recorded sound source at a particular position in the stereo field.

Patch change. *See* **Program change**.

Pedal. A sustained or repeated note against which changing chords are heard.

Phantom image. A sound image generated by amplitude panning so that it emanates from between two stereo speakers rather than directly from a single speaker.

Phantom power. 12 to 48v DC applied to pins 2 and 3 of the microphone connector through two equal resistors. It is required to make non-electret condenser microphones work and is usually supplied from the mic input of the mixing desk.

Phase cancellation. An undesirable effect where interference is caused by the same sound being picked up by two spaced microphones and mixed together. One signal will be slightly out of time with the other and the interference that results often cancels out much of the body of the sound. Phase cancellation can also occur when recording vocals if there are reflective surfaces close to the microphone and the vocalist.

Phasing. A gently undulating delay effect in which the delay-time is gradually changed.

Piano-roll. A style of graphical editing screen within a software sequencer. Based on the punched-paper piano-roll which was fed into a player piano to produce an automatic peformance.

Pitch. The perceived depth or height of a note, based on the frequency of the vibrations producing it.

Pitch bend. (1) A deviation in the pitch of a note, used for expressive effect in pop music and jazz. (2) The MIDI message for inflecting the pitch, up or down, of all the notes on a given MIDI channel.

Pitch shift. A sound transformation technique which alters the pitch of a recorded audio track without changing its speed.

Pizzicato. Plucked – a technique used by string players instead of bowing the strings.

Polyphonic. Capable of playing many notes at the same time.

Polyrhythm. The simultaneous use of two or more conflicting rhythms.

Pop shield. A device to stop air from a singer's mouth directly hitting a microphone, causing a popping sound.

Preamp. An electronic circuit and the first stage of amplification used to boost a signal level. Found in the input stages of mixing desks for boosting mic levels, also as external standalone units, in guitar amplifiers and as part of the internal workings of a condenser microphone.

Program change. A MIDI message that indicates the selection of a new sound (or voice) on a particular MIDI channel.

Programme music. Music intended to invoke extra-musical images, such as suggesting a scene or narrative of events.

Proximity effect. The bass boost that occurs when using a cardioid microphone placed close to a sound source. The closer the mic, the greater the low-frequency boost.

Punch in/out. A method of re-recording or overdubbing a specific section of a track by hitting a button or pedal when the section begins (punch-in or drop-in) and ends (punch-out or drop-out).

Quantise. On sequencers the process of automatically adjusting data to fit within defined limits. Commonly used to shift note-starts to (or nearer to) their rhythmically exact positions, although it can also be used to modify note-lengths and velocity levels.

Real time. Operations which are carried out without delay, eg as the music is playing.

Reverb. Short for reverberation. The complex series of reflections that occurs when sound is made in an enclosed space. Often artificially added to a recording – originally by mechanical spring or plate devices, but now more commonly produced digitally. *See also* **echo**.

Riff. A term commonly used in pop and jazz to indicate a repeated musical phrase. *See also* **ostinato**.

Rubato. Literally robbed time. Expressive changes to the position of beats within a bar, sometimes leading to expressive fluctuations in the overall tempo (common in some types of romantic music).

Sampler. A device for recording sections of sound (samples) and allowing them to be played back at different speeds.

Scale. A series of notes in ascending (or descending) order. The type of scale (eg major, minor, blues) is determined by the order of the tone and semitone gaps between the notes.

Semitone. Half a **tone**. The smallest commonly used interval in western tonal music (eg from E to F, or F to F♯).

Sequence. (1) Musical performance data recorded on a sequencer. Also used as a verb (to sequence) meaning to produce a sequence. (2) The *immediate* repetition at a different pitch of a phrase or motif in a continuous melodic line.

Sequencer. A device (or computer software) for the input, editing, storage and play-back of musical performance data using (at least in the last 20 years) MIDI. Sequencers may include other facilities, such as the ability to convert performance data to music notation or to combine sampled sounds with MIDI data.

Shuffle rhythm. A rhythm formed from **swing quavers** played at a moderate speed and in a **legato** style.

SMF. Standard MIDI file (*see* **MIDI file.**)

SMPTE. A standard timing code (in hours, minutes, seconds and frames) used in the synchronisation of sound and music to moving pictures. The letters are an acronym for the Society of Motion Picture and Television Engineers who invented it.

Software. A computer program – a series of instructions which determines how the hardware of a computer will respond.

Speaker. Abbreviation of **loudspeaker**.

Spot-mic. A microphone placed close to an instrument in order to pick up detail, or to record weaker instruments in an ensemble.

Staccato. Detached. Short notes, often shown in music notation by dots above or below the notes affected. The opposite of **legato**.

Step time. A method of entering note values in free time into a sequencer, which then generates the playback timing.

Stereo. An abbreviation of stereophonic. The use of two audio tracks to represent a solid sound image (stereo is Greek for solid), reflecting the way that humans perceive sounds through two ears.

Stereo panning. The position (left to right) of a sound in stereo.

Sustain pedal. Device on a piano for allowing notes to continue to sound after the keys have been released. MIDI controller 64 is used to emulate this feature.

Swing quavers. The division of the beat into a pair of notes in which the first is longer than the second. In music notation swing quavers are often written as shown in the first two examples, *right*, but are performed as shown in the third example.

Syncopation. Off-beat accents or accents on weak beats.

Synthesiser. A device which generates sounds electronically.

System message. A category of MIDI message which is either used for synchronising many devices together (eg **MTC**) or for sending information that is specific to the equipment of one manufacturer.

Tempo. The speed of the underlying beat in a piece of music. This may be indicated by a general description (eg fast, or allegro) or it may be shown by a precise speed expressed in **bpm** or given as a **metronome** mark.

Timbre. The quality that makes one sound (eg of a flute) different from another (eg a trumpet) even though both may be playing the same pitch at the same volume. Timbre results from complex sound waves and even one instrument can change the timbre of a note by using by such methods as varying the attack and dynamic level, or by using different methods of note production (eg by plucking a violin instead of bowing it, or by using a mute).

Time signature. Numbers at the start of a passage of music which show the pattern of beats that make up a bar. For instance $\frac{4}{4}$ indicates four crotchets (or quarter-notes) per bar, while $\frac{3}{8}$ indicates three quavers (or eighth-notes) per bar. **C** is another way of writing $\frac{4}{4}$ and **₵** is the equivalent of $\frac{2}{2}$.

Tone. (1) Two semitones (eg from C to D). (2) The quality of a note (eg a harsh tone) which is often used on amplifiers or mixers as a sets of tone controls for **EQ**.

Track. A part of a sequencer or recording that is used to store one or more discrete elements of the full texture, such as a drum track on a sequencer or, on two-track stereo, the data for each of the two channels (left and right).

Transpose. To move all the notes in a passage of music up or down by the same amount. This will change the key unless the transposition is by 12 semitones, which will merely change the octave.

Two-track. An audio recording that uses two tracks of sound, usually to produce stereo.

Velocity. The measure of how fast a keyboard key was pressed. This is used in MIDI to determine the loudness of a note and often (but indirectly) its timbre and attack.

Vibrato. Small but repeating fluctuations in pitch used by performers to give warmth and expression to their tone.

Volume. The loudness of a sound, particularly in reference to the sound intensity control on an amplifier or mixer.

Waveform. A sound signal which has a particular shape (especially when displayed on an oscilloscope or in a sound-editing program).

Wav file. A commonly used file for storing digital audio information, particularly on PC-based computers.

Further information

The Studio Musician's Jargonbuster by Godric Wilkie. *Musonix/Music Sales* (1993). ISBN: 0-9517214-2-9. A glossary of 1,500 terms used in music technology and recording.

See also the following web-based glossaries:

www.rane.com/digi-dic.html
www.audioc.com/information/audio_glossary/glossary.html
www.recordingeq.com/reflib.html